Contents

Part I
Building A Rock Solid Foundation Of A Professional LinkedIn Profile

Do You Make These Mistakes in Your LinkedIn Profile?

I have put together a list of the most common mistakes people make when it comes to their LinkedIn profile. It will give you a good head start and also save you valuable time and effort. There are many other mistakes and issues I will be tackling throughout the book; however the 12 listed below are the most obvious ones almost every LinkedIn user will, at one point or another, come across.

Vague LinkedIn headline

People put their business title here and leave it at that. Now, this could be seriously costly. Why would I want to connect to you or read any further down your profile if you don't engage me here?

The LinkedIn headline is one of the most important features of your profile and you must make full use of its power. It gets you attention; it shows your value and boosts your visibility.

The profile written in third person

This is so common. Users talk about themselves and it sounds as if they are describing a stranger. Why would you step back and get someone else to describe you and your services? It makes it very impersonal – don't do it!

Missing photograph

Perception is everything. I want to connect to the real person, not to someone invisible. My reaction would be that you either have something to hide or do not take your business seriously. LinkedIn is a business to business directory and a photograph is a must. By having no photo on your profile you will miss out on opportunities.

Incomplete information

You know your business inside out but you haven't filled out all of your profile. There are big gaps, missing pieces, sketchy details and one line descriptions. How am I to get to know you and what you do from a partial profile? You are not helping potential prospects or anyone looking at your profile to understand what you have to offer and how you can help.

No LinkedIn summary

Without the summary section there is no introduction and welcome to you as a professional and the services you offer. People would end up going straight to the experience section which doesn't have the same impact.

Missing contact details

Make it easy for your people to contact you by adding a telephone number so potential clients can get hold of you easily. Don't just redirect me to your website where I have to dig out your contact details. I have never been pestered by anyone on LinkedIn with unsolicited calls.

No LinkedIn recommendations

Having no recommendations means you have no third party evidence telling the world you can do what you say you can do. I have only your word for that on your profile. By having other people endorsing you and say how good you are at what you do, it encourages trust much, much more.

Wrong LinkedIn skills and expertise keywords

LinkedIn's featured skills and endorsements are searchable words on your profile, and by having the wrong words you complicate people's understanding of what you do. Many use random words that have nothing to do with their business – remove them and use the right ones.

Lack of personal details

I find that including personal information softens your profile and makes you more approachable and interesting to others as a real person.

Not belonging to LinkedIn groups

Raising visibility on LinkedIn is no mean feat. By joining groups you can communicate effectively with smaller hubs of people and become more visible locally or in your target market. What's more, if you contribute in active group conversations, you will be perceived as an expert in your field.

Hard sell approach

No one wants to be sold to. You make a new connection and before even speaking to them you send them your price list and brochure. Why would you do that? You run the risk of turning people off before you have found out if they need your services. Don't lose that sale!

Blind self-promotion

There are many ways to blow your own trumpet; non-stop self-promotion isn't one of them. It's boring and, quite frankly, who cares how fantastic you are? I do find it amusing when people say they are gurus, evangelists, entrepreneurs and so on. These emotive words mean different things to different people. All marketing strategies need to appeal and add value to your target market; it's not all about you.

These are the basic starting points to building your LinkedIn profile and avoiding the most obvious mistakes – some you may already know, some not. Hopefully they give you a different perspective on your LinkedIn profile.

Points one to nine will be covered in Chapter 1; the point about LinkedIn groups in Chapter 10; the hard sell approach in Chapter 3; and developing marketing strategies in Chapter 7 will deal with self-promotion. Once we have put together a fantastic LinkedIn profile, you can start creating a bespoke sales and marketing strategy and, as a result, all the time investment you have put in will come to fruition.

1

Eight Steps to Create an All Star LinkedIn Profile

Your personal profile representing you and your business is at the very heart of LinkedIn. Putting together a powerful LinkedIn profile that is unique to you is the first step to generating tremendous success for you and your business. In this chapter I will cover all the elements crucial to your LinkedIn profile so people can clearly see who you are, what you do and stand for and, ultimately, how you can help them.

If your LinkedIn profile isn't complete and doesn't outline what there is to know about you both as a person and as a professional, or if it is not engaging you will be missing many opportunities coming your way and your LinkedIn activity will be wasted.

I will be taking you through your profile one step at a time aiming to appeal to prospective clients in a way they would want to connect and do business with you. What's more, this chapter will help lay the groundwork for creating a top notch professional profile to make you stand out from the crowd big time and give you an edge over your competition.

Getting Started with Your LinkedIn Profile

A LinkedIn profile can be used in two ways: as a CV to find a job and boost your career; or as a sales tool to grow your business. You will need a different approach for each; and it all starts with building an effective personal yet professional LinkedIn profile.

There are five levels of profile strength you go through as a new LinkedIn user to build up and complete your LinkedIn profile in order to make full use of it.

1. Beginner

2. Intermediate

3. Advanced

4. Expert

5. All-Star

By completing all your LinkedIn profile sections correctly you will achieve the strongest All-Star LinkedIn profile level giving you that extra visibility and adding massive confidence in you and your services.

Your LinkedIn profile needs to reflect back what your target market wants to see. This is because when people search for you and your services their first thought and approach is, "What's In It For Me?" (also known as WIIFM).

Are potential clients going to be interested in you straight away? No, they are interested in helping themselves. They need to see clearly, specifically and at a glance if you are able to help them and how, so you must make it easy for them to see this with the information you have on display throughout your profile.

I will explain the process of how to complete your profile from top to bottom and the reasons why, and on completion your personality and professionalism will shine through. Only then can we start planning a strategy together that will work for you to get new sales, trump your competition and turn you into a leader in your area of expertise.

First of all, you need to sign up to LinkedIn and set up a personal profile if you don't have one yet. It's easy to do, go to www.linkedin.com and follow the steps on the LinkedIn platform and then come back to get started with the next step.

1: Choosing the Right LinkedIn Profile Photo to Portray You Best at a Glance

The first thing people get to see on your LinkedIn profile and your activity is your photograph. So, first of all, please avoid being the invisible person by having no photograph on your profile. Perception is reality, and by having no photo at all you might come across as having something to hide or you are not a confident person. Also, did you know that adding a photograph on your LinkedIn profile increases your visibility by at least 11 times?

Your photograph needs to be a recent head and shoulders professional shot to create that crucial first impression, which has to be a good one. There's no need to stress about wrinkles. Your photo on the computer screen is only three centimetres wide so no one can see the wrinkles if there are any. Does it matter if it is an older or more recent photo? I'd say go with the most up to date photo.

It is best to avoid using a holiday snap or family shot or party photograph. LinkedIn is Business-to-Business (B2B) communication and interaction so you should think in terms of you being the face of your business. Are you, therefore, giving the right and making an impactful impression? People buy from people so what they want to see is the real and down to earth person they are connecting to. This is why you shouldn't use a logo either; the place to use a logo is on your company page.

Here's how to add your photograph.

Along the top black bar of your LinkedIn screen, click on the word "**Me**". On the drop down menu click "**View profile**". Click the blue pencil next to the "**More...**" button. You will be taken to a new window where you can upload a new photograph by clicking the blue pencil next to the photo circle. Once uploaded, drag the photo into position and use the slider to enlarge or reduce your image to fit the circle.

You need to make your profile as visible as possible. Click on the **"Visibility"** wording (just above the **"Apply"** button) and make sure your profile settings are set to public. Then click the blue **"Save"** button to make the changes.

Consider wearing corporate clothing or having your logo in the background for brand reinforcement when taking a photo. A bright background colour also helps you to stand out. I am not a fan of black and white photographs because they tend to make your image blend with and fade into the background on the computer screen.

Furthermore, though you might have a good sense of humour, I would avoid using illustrations or caricatures, because it could create the perception you don't take your business activity seriously.

If you don't want to alert your network, click first on the button to "**No, don't update my network**" and then click the blue "**Save**" button. However, I would suggest going for updating your network as it increases visibility and helps you get noticed more on LinkedIn.

2: How to Craft an Eye-Catching LinkedIn Profile Headline

The LinkedIn profile headline is one of the most important parts of your whole LinkedIn profile for three reasons. One, it facilitates search as it is the first place LinkedIn starts searching when people type a keyword. Two, it increases visibility because it uses keywords to boost the search process to gain more visibility and be found. Three, it adds value as it grabs attention and appeals to your target market.

Your LinkedIn headline is the first place LinkedIn start with the search algorithm. Similar to search engine optimization (SEO) to help get onto page one of Google, for example, if you don't have your relevant keywords describing your services included in your headline you are making it harder for potential clients to find you.

People need to see, at the click of a finger, the value you bring to the table.

Remember, prospects will always be thinking of themselves first, so you need to engage them straight away with a specific skill and benefit loaded LinkedIn profile headline.

However, what you don't want to have in your headline is just your title or a list of searchable words. Follow this simple layout to create a powerful professional headline in three easy to follow stages:

• Describe what you do

• Specify the value you bring

• Include searchable keywords relating to your business and services

You have up to 120 available characters in your headline including spaces, so you need to be concise and precise and get the attention of your target client in one sentence.

This is not an easy task. It might take a few sheets of paper to get it right but keep going at it, try different headlines and you will make it happen.

If you don't have an engaging, benefit loaded headline people will not want to read the rest of your profile meaning you could be losing out on new opportunities. It is also worth pointing out that whatever activity you are doing on LinkedIn, your profile headline is on display and follows you everywhere. Here's how this works:

Whenever you post an update on the Home page on LinkedIn, what people see first is your profile photograph and next to it your name and your headline. Similarly, if you add a comment or start a discussion in LinkedIn groups, again, what people see first is your photograph, your name and your headline. You now get the picture.

Let's take my headline as an example. My search words are "LinkedIn Training" and "LinkedIn Workshops" and my value proposition is in, *"Helping Sales Teams connect to their next biggest client & generate more profit."* This is because I am focussed on the end result of my activity instead of compiling an impersonal list of services.

You want to get attention in a positive way to encourage people interested in your services to read on. Remember, their motto is,*"What's in it for me?"* or *"How can I benefit by buying your services?"* Specify therefore the value you bring into their hands.

Here's how to change your LinkedIn profile headline.

Along the top black bar of your LinkedIn screen, click on the word "**Me**". On the drop down menu click "**View profile**". Click on the blue pencil on the right hand side of your screen and start typing in the headline box. Click the blue "**Save**" button when completed.

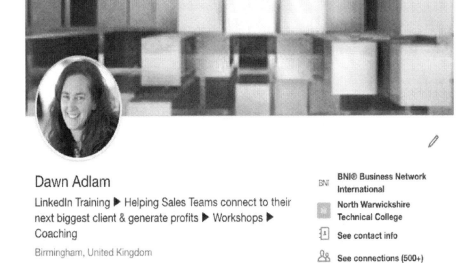

Dawn Adlam

LinkedIn Training ▶ Helping Sales Teams connect to their next biggest client & generate profits ▶ Workshops ▶ Coaching

Birmingham, United Kingdom

BNI® Business Network International

North Warwickshire Technical College

See contact info

See connections (500+)

Change your LinkedIn profile headline to best represent your activity. For example, if you wanted to create a particular strategy aimed at HR professionals then you can use that value statement in your headline. In this way your HR connections can see straight away how you can help them. For example, *"I support HR professionals to…,"* or if you want to connect to accountants then the value statement could be, *"Helping Accountants to…"* and so on. You can change your headline as often as you want to so you can adapt this to your strategy and activity.

Booster Tip: If you add an icon to your headline, make sure there is a space before and after the icon, otherwise the word will not be recognised in LinkedIn searches.

3: How to Choose a Unique Public LinkedIn Profile for Your Brand

A crucial part of your LinkedIn profile is your personal URL, which stands for Unique Reference Link. Your URL is unique to you on LinkedIn, and there is only one URL profile per person allowed within LinkedIn.

The URL default setting has a list of numbers which is messy and confusing. The URL needs to be personalised to you as it makes it easier for you to be searched for and found. This is also a little touch that neatens your personal LinkedIn profile. You can then have your business cards printed including your unique LinkedIn URL. Here's how to create a personalised URL:

Along the top black bar of your LinkedIn screen, click on the word "**Me**". On the drop down menu click "**View profile**". On the right hand side of the new screen, click on the grey text "**Edit public profile & URL**". This takes you to another screen where, on the top right hand side you can change your details by clicking the blue pencil and adding the **URL** . Your details need to be your name and surname, all in lowercase and with no spaces.

Edit public profile & URL

See and edit how you look to people who are not signed in, and find you through search engines (ex: Google, Bing).

If there are already users on LinkedIn with the same name as yours (there are over 16,000 Rob Smiths!), LinkedIn will make suggestions for you and you can choose to add a number at the end of the line or reversing your first name and surname or adding a middle name. Click the blue **"Save"** button when the unique name is added.

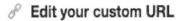

🔗 Edit your custom URL

Personalize the URL for your profile.

www.linkedin.com/in/dawnadlam

Note: Your custom URL must contain 3-100 letters
or numbers. Please do not use spaces, symbols, or
special characters.

Cancel **Save**

Some LinkedIn users choose to remain anonymous (I am not sure why they would want to be on LinkedIn and choose to do this!). Should you wish to do so you can become anonymous at any time by using the Customise Your Public Profile section. Here's how.

Along the top black bar of your LinkedIn screen, click on the word "**Me**". On the drop down, menu click "**View profile**". On the right hand side of the new screen, click on the grey text "**Edit public profile & URL**".

On the new screen, about half way down, under the wording Edit Visibility, click the blue "**On**" button next to the "**Your profile's public visibility**" wording. It might be that you want to do some market research or look at your competitors. However, remember to repeat the process and click back on being visible after you are done.

◎ Edit Visibility

You control your profile's appearance for viewers who are not logged-in members. Limits you set here affect how your profile appears on search engines, profile badges, and permitted services like Outlook.
Learn more

Your profile's public visibility   On

LinkedIn is an open forum, and you should make full use of your public profile by being completely visible and transparent. The more you do so the more easily you will be found by potential clients. In terms of improving visibility you want to be open to engage with as many people as you can; some people will connect with you, some won't. But by remaining invisible and having only a few connections you will have a limited outreach. Here's how to make your profile fully visible.

Along the top black bar of your LinkedIn screen, click on the word "**Me**". On the drop down menu click "**View profile**". On the right hand side click on the grey text "**Edit your public profile & URL**". On the new screen under the Public button make sure all the elements are ticked to "**Show**".

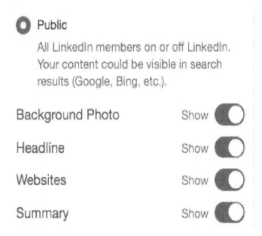

Here you can also create a custom LinkedIn profile badge to add onto your website, blog, email footers, marketing materials and so on. This is a unique *"View my profile on LinkedIn"* button which makes it very easy for people to find you. All they have to do is click on the button and will be taken directly to your LinkedIn profile without having to spend time searching for it. Here's how.

On the same page, right at the bottom, underneath the wording Public Profile badge click the blue "**Create a badge**" button. On the new screen, follow the steps provided and choose the badge you prefer from the options available. Each sample badge comes with a developer code, which you or your web developer can copy and add accordingly.

4: How to Present Yourself Professionally and Honestly in the LinkedIn Profile About Section

Once interest has been generated from your unique and professional LinkedIn profile headline, an introduction and an overview of what you offer comes into play in your LinkedIn About section. This is your personal introductory statement. Focus on WHAT drives you and WHY you choose the profession you are in. This is not the place to list your services and products, because no one will care about that until they buy into the real you. Who wants to read a shopping list, anyway?

Start with an introduction sentence such as " *Thank you for viewing my profile*". Understand the needs and concerns of your audience and reflect back in your About section the details your target market wants to find out and know more about. WHO do you help and HOW? WHY you are on LinkedIn and what the real value you bring would be.

Always have a call to action near the end of the About section. How can people buy from you – what happens next? It could be an offer for a complimentary assessment, a free initial meeting or a no obligation phone or skype call.

You have up to 2000 words in here. Don't bore people with too much information; life is too short to wade through paragraph after paragraph – aim for no more than four or five paragraphs – often, if done properly, less is more.

LinkedIn searches your About section for relevant keywords in your field of business, so add at least six different keywords for more visibility. If you offer more than one service, create a short paragraph for each service so you can cross sell and also add additional keywords that are not included in your headline. This helps in being far more visible in the searches within LinkedIn, and your connections can clearly see what services are relevant to them.

For example, if you are a web design company you can have an introduction saying you are on LinkedIn to help businesses gain more visibility and generate more sales. Have separate paragraphs including keywords on Web Design, Branding, SEO, e Commerce, Pay Per Click and so on. However, avoid repeating the same keywords too often. Why not offer a free website health check and add your contact number if you want people to call you? You can change and update your summary as often as you like to keep in order to keep it relevant and up to date. Here's how to add it.

Along the top black bar of your LinkedIn screen, click on the word "**Me**". On the drop down, menu click "**View profile**". Click on the blue pencil on the right hand side of **"About"** and start typing in the box. Making sure to space the paragraphs out for easy reading, but note that you cannot change the size or the font type. Click the blue "**Save**" button when completed.

Booster Tip: Create your About draft in a Word document first, and make sure you correct spelling mistakes and grammar as they make your profile look very untidy and unprofessional.

5: The Secrets of Using Skills & Endorsements Effectively to Prove Your Expertise

This section of your LinkedIn profile provides a snapshot of your services in one or a combination of more than one keyword, all of which are searchable and help increase your visibility further. Decide which words and phrases best describe your services and add them. As these words and phrases are clicked on and endorsed by other people in your network they will appear in the most popular order.

You can add up to 50 Skills & Endorsement words. LinkedIn does make suggestions on popular words to use, but if the keywords you want aren't suggested you can add your own.

I was recently hired by an Independent Financial Advisor expert who wanted to add all 50 words (it took quite some time to do). We did this and, as a result, the following week he picked up his first client through LinkedIn. The client checked the IFA's profile and saw that he could help them with everything they needed.

Working towards achieving a complete LinkedIn profile you need to have at least 25 endorsements, and to get there my advice would be to add 30 relevant keywords and phrases that best describe your products and services. Spending time endorsing your 1st line connections would also help.

To add your Skills words, go along the top black bar of your LinkedIn screen and click on the word "**Me**". On the drop down menu click "**View profile**".

Scroll down the page until you come to the Skills & Endorsements section (located underneath the Volunteering section). Click the "**Add a new skill**" text and add your keywords. Click the blue "**Save**" button to add them.

To reorder or remove the keywords, click on the blue pencil on the right hand side next to the "**Add a new skill**" text. On the new screen, click on the four parallel grey line symbol on the right hand side of each keyword and drag up or down to your preferred order. To remove a keyword, click on the "**X**" on the left hand side of it and it will disappear. Click the blue "**Save**" button.

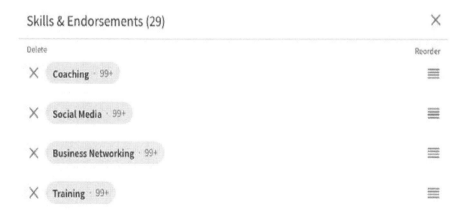

In each section you can choose the priority order by clicking the pin icon next to each word. But, make sure your best skills, at least your top three, are displayed first.

To change the order click the blue pin of the word you want to remove then click on the pin of the word you want to be displayed in the top three.

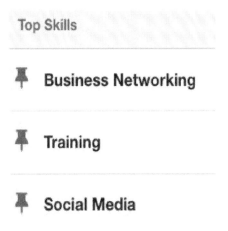

If you have not added any keywords to your profile click the **"Add profile section"** button and click **"Skills"** to add them. Remember to click the blue **"Save"** button to add them to your profile.

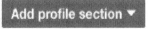

While you are here removing or reordering keywords, you can adjust your endorsement settings by clicking on the **"Adjust endorsement settings"** text located on the left hand side of the blue Save button. There are three options to choose from.

Your 1st line connections can click on the blue "+" icon next to each word to endorse you. You can do the same for your connections. Click the "+" icon, rate your connection's skills as Good, Very good or Highly skilled, select the relationship you have with them and then click the blue **"Submit"** button.

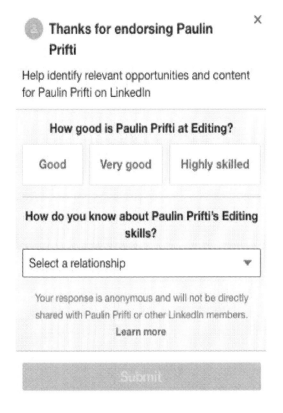

This is a validation of your services and skills as the people you know and have worked with can use this to endorse you. You cannot endorse yourself, therefore this section backs up and provides social proof of what you say you can do, all coming from people other than yourself.

One or two endorsements are easy to obtain but having 99+ people endorsing you makes a far better impression and cements your credibility. Having 99+ endorsements alongside the top ten skills words is what you should aim for.

I know, it will take time to reach 99+ endorsements but go for it because it will make a massive difference. Aim for at least 50 endorsements per skill to start with.

Coaching · 99+

Remember, being endorsed only by people you know and trust shows integrity. There is no benefit in endorsing people if you can't personally vouch for them. There is also no point in having endorsements for services you don't offer, it is confusing. If you are endorsed for skills that are not relevant to you (it happens quite often) just remove them. Here's how.

Along the top black bar of your LinkedIn screen, click on the word "**Me**". On the drop down menu click "**View profile**". Scroll down until you come to the Skills & Endorsements section (underneath the Volunteering section). Click on the blue pencil next to the wording "**Add a new skill**".

Featured Skills & Endorsements   Add a new skill ✎

Your list of words will appear, click on the dustbin icon on the right hand side to remove the word. Click "**Save**" when done.

Business Networking

Training

Social Media

It is good to invest time endorsing others whom you know and would recommend, they would appreciate the effort and you end up becoming visible on their profile. Make this a regular weekly activity as it leads to extra visibility within LinkedIn, too.

6: How to Use the LinkedIn Experience Section to Show the Full Depth of Your Skills

Now you need to start filling in the gaps of your experience both in the past and now. When completing these sections, think about the expertise and knowledge you have and how they are relevant to a potential customer. Take care not to add too much detail here as you can do this in your headline and summary sections. This section is more about your personal experience within a particular role to enable you to show the range of your skills and expertise in that position.

Add your job history as far back as you are comfortable with. However, having had ten jobs in ten years might not give the best impression as it may come across you move around continually and cannot settle in a job. In such a case show only the last five positions. Don't worry if you have taken time out to have children or for a career break, no one will be analysing in too much detail.

You will notice that the headline in your LinkedIn experience section is in bold. The words you use here are also searchable titles; which is why you need to use new and specific words describing your experience. Avoid using just generic words such as Director, CEO and so on. Separate the words with a slash but leave a space on each side of the symbol (/), so the actual words can be picked up and searched for easily.

Experience

 Bizlinks Coach / Social Media Training / LinkedIn Training / Lead Generation
TheBizlinks
Feb 2012 – Present • 5 yrs 1 mo • West Midlands

For example, I use the words "Bizlinks Coach", "Social Media Training", "LinkedIn Training" and "Lead Generation" (Bizlinks Coach / Social Media Training / LinkedIn Training / Lead Generation and not Bizlinks Coach/Social Media Training/LinkedIn Training/Lead Generation). They are additional searchable keywords relating to my services I haven't used in my LinkedIn headline or about sections.

Pull in your corporate logos here for each individual experience section to increase brand awareness. If the company you worked or work for have a LinkedIn company page (see chapter 8 on company pages) then add its logo directly to your profile. If you have worked for well-known companies or brands remember to advertise them on your LinkedIn profile, because displaying them will add further to your credibility.

People can click on the logo and will be taken directly to the company page, which serves as your website within the LinkedIn platform. Here's how to add the logo.

Along the top black bar of your LinkedIn screen, click on the word "**Me**". On the drop down menu click "**View profile**". Scroll down your profile to the Experience section and click on the blue pencil on the right hand side. A new window titled Edit experience will pop up.

Edit experience   ✕

Title

Bizlinks Coach / Social Media Training / LinkedIn Training / Lead Generation

Company

TheBizlinks

Location

West Midlands

In the Company section delete the company name if it is already there without the logo being displayed and start typing your company name (just start typing the company name if nothing has been added here). LinkedIn will automatically recognise the link to the company page and will make suggestions for you.

If there is a choice of different logos, select the correct one and LinkedIn will position the logo on the left hand side of your profile. Click the blue **"Save"** button. Repeat this for all your past positions you want to have on display.

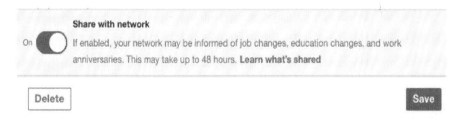

Share with network

On   If enabled, your network may be informed of job changes, education changes, and work anniversaries. This may take up to 48 hours. **Learn what's shared**

Delete   Save

If the company page has been set up without a logo then you cannot add a logo. See Chapter 8 on setting up a company page then repeat as above. You want that recognition of working with a good brand and also the opportunity to showcase your business within LinkedIn.

We're nearly there; let's put the final touches to your profile.

7: Getting Raving LinkedIn Recommendations

from Your Clients and Differentiate Yourself from the Competition

"What people say about you is hundred times more powerful that what you say about yourself," Zig Ziglar once said.

I cannot emphasise enough how important what clients say about you is. Having testimonials from your clients saying how you helped them, what a great job you did, how you saved the day, how much money you saved them and so on, is a major scoring point on your professional LinkedIn profile.

Having two or three recommendations is ok. But having 20 plus boosts your credibility immensely because, firstly, your peers recognise your great work and, secondly, it helps you get noticed by backing up your value statements.

Always ask for recommendations from customers, suppliers, colleagues or strategic alliances to show a cross section of all your services and your expertise. To give or receive a recommendation you must be connected on LinkedIn to the person you want to give to or receive a recommendation from. There are two ways to ask for a recommendation.

The first is via your own profile. Along the top black bar of your LinkedIn screen, click on the word "**Me**". On the drop down menu click "**View profile**", then scroll down to your Recommendations section, which you'll find near the bottom of your own LinkedIn profile.

Click on the blue pencil on the right hand side of the text "**Ask to be recommended**". In the new window that pops up, follow these four simple steps to ask for a recommendation.

First, select the person you want to ask to recommend you. Ask one person at a time as it is more of a personal request rather than in bulk, and it only takes a couple minutes to do.

Second, select your relationship with that person.

Third, choose the role you want to be recommended for (the recommendation will automatically show in that experience section).

Fourth, send a personal message asking to be recommended.

Booster Tip: This will save you time when asking for recommendations. Write out your personal message in a Word document or Evernote first, and make sure to leave enough space in the middle of the request for three questions to guide the person write a recommendation based on your values.

Type out a list of ten questions you can cut and paste from, questions which have relevance to the person you are asking and will guide them with their response. I always ask at the end of the personal message for a recommendation the question, *"Would you recommend me to your clients?"*

Let's take an example. You are a Financial Advisor and you saved your client money. Ask how much money your client saved using your services over a particular period of time. Be specific and relate the questions to the information provided on your profile headline and summary.

When the recommendation has been made by your connection you will be asked if you want to add it to your profile. Please always proofread and check any grammatical errors and typos as they make your profile look very unprofessional. If there are any, click "**Ask for revision**" and ask for amendments.

The second way to ask for a recommendation is directly from your 1st line connection. Go to the profile of the person you want to ask for a recommendation and, under their photograph, click on the "**More…**" button on the right hand side of the **"Message"** button.

Then on the drop-down menu that appears click "**Request a Recommendation**". Follow the same instructions as above in asking them recommend you. Again, proofread and double check there are no typos when you receive the recommendation before accepting and adding it to your LinkedIn profile.

To have a fully completed LinkedIn profile you need a minimum of two LinkedIn recommendations from others on your profile. Remember to be authentic and only ask for recommendations from people you are connected to and have genuinely worked with or done business together. If someone I haven't worked with asks me for a recommendation I politely decline.

Also, it is important to balance out the giving and receiving of recommendations as it would look rather selfish and one sided to have received 20, for example, and have given none in return.

You should make recommending others a priority. Use this simple way to give a recommendation.

Go to the profile of the person you want to recommend and under their photograph, click on the "**More**…" button on the right hand side of the Message button. On the drop down menu click "**Recommend**" and follow the instructions. Write and send the recommendation and once the person accepts it, your recommendation you will be visible on their profile.

Recommendations are seen as social proof on your profile and really do boost your credibility on a personal and professional level. I recently gained a new customer as they said they were talking to two LinkedIn trainers but when they saw all my glowing recommendations they gave me the business.

So set yourself the task of asking for and giving at least 20 to start with and keep adding them regularly. Aim for at least 50 good quality recommendations, that will really make you stand out big time against your competition.

8: Highlighting Your Credentials Better

Depending upon what stage of your career you are in, you can go into as much or as little detail about your education in this section. Where are you on your career journey? How important is it to a new employer to see where you were educated and your qualifications?

If you are just starting out in your career it would warrant more detail especially if you are looking for your first job. If you have been 20 years in business and school was a long time ago then it is not so relevant. Either way, you will need to add some detail to this section in order to round up and complete your LinkedIn profile to All Star status.

Consider the list below and if any of them are relevant at this moment in time then complete them in this order:

• School

• Degree

• Field

• Grade

• Activities and societies

• Dates you studied

Don't sweat over the exact dates or the description. It is a long time since I went to school, that's why I have included my college dates rather than the senior school ones. Here's how to add education.

Along the top black bar of your LinkedIn screen, click on the word **"Me"**. On the drop down menu click **"View profile"**. Scroll down your profile and in the Education section click the blue **"+"** button and enter the details. Click the blue **"Save"** button when completed.

Education   +

North Warwickshire Technical College
NNEB, English Language, English Literature
1982 – 1984

/

If there are any sections of your profile that you have not added yet, you can find and add them by clicking on the blue **"Add profile section"** button, which you'll see on the right hand side of your headline.

Phew! Well done, that's part one of creating an outstanding and unique LinkedIn profile for getting that all important extra visibility. One small yet immensely vital part of reaching a top level professional status is to work towards building a minimum of 50 connections in your network. More on that later in the book.

Now let's move on to taking your profile up another gear and be prepared to be amazed at what else you can include and have on display on your LinkedIn profile.

The crucial thing to do next is to start to drive traffic to your profile – the more new contacts looking at your profile the better as they could easily become new clients by using a simple yet effective conversation tactic.

2

Six Steps to Sharpen Your LinkedIn Profile

So far we have covered creating your LinkedIn profile in its basic form. Yet, your profile can do so much more than just introducing you and your services. Taking your LinkedIn profile and activity to the next level of excellence is similar to putting together a jigsaw puzzle; there are more pieces to add to complete the picture and maximise the many opportunities LinkedIn can offer.

At this particular stage of your LinkedIn professional activity, attention to detail makes all the difference. What I am going to share with you from now on is inside knowledge and valuable time saving social media tips to streamline your business. There are behind the scenes tips you'll learn that will make your LinkedIn profile so much more appealing, which in turn will attract new prospects to you.

You'll be able to do so much more with the strategy I have laid out in this chapter. For example, if you have or can create marketing material about you and your business you can use Slideshare to share it online and drive floods of traffic to your website. Use this strategy and your LinkedIn presence will spike and attract increasing interest towards you and what you stand for and carve a massive route to market and boost your future sales.

1: How to Make it Easy for Clients Who Want to Do Business to Contact You

Let's look at your contact information located on the right hand side of your LinkedIn profile page. Visible to all your 1st line LinkedIn connections will be: your LinkedIn URL; the three website call to action lines section; your phone number, email address, Twitter, Skype and birthday details depending on how many of these you have entered.

Add a telephone number if you want people to call you. I know it sounds obvious, but it would save people valuable time especially if they are trying to get hold of you. Your email address also sits here and it needs to be a business email address, because using a personal email address can create the wrong impression: are you doing this as a serious business or just a hobby?

However, it is wise to add your personal email address, especially if you are an employee. If you change jobs you can log back into your LinkedIn profile to make the necessary new changes and updates using your personal email address. Otherwise, you will be locked out of your profile if you can't use your business email address anymore. To sort this out, you would need to ask LinkedIn's Help Centre to unlock your LinkedIn profile and this is time consuming. Make your new business email your primary email address and, therefore, visible to your connections adding further to your credibility.

Here's how to make changes to your contact information.

Along the top black bar of your LinkedIn screen, click on the word **"Me"**. On the drop down menu click **"View profile"**. On the left hand side of your screen, underneath your headline click the text **"Contact Info"** and you will be taken to a new screen.

Shirley, West Midlands, United Kingdom
Contact info

It is then straightforward to change your contact details, first click on the blue pencil and then amend each section.

Dawn Adlam

Contact Info

 Your Profile

linkedin.com/in/dawnadlam

 Websites

thebizlinks.com/contact/ (20 minute sales call)

bni-phoenix.co.uk (Looking to Network?)

bnibirmingham.com/en-GB/index (Looking for New Business?)

Phone

07880725564 (Work)

Make sure you click the blue **"Save"** button to save all the changes. To change your email address, you need to go into you Settings and Privacy hub. Along the top black bar of your LinkedIn screen, click on the word **"Me"**. On the dropdown menu then click **"Settings and Privacy"**.

Basics

Email addresses   Change

Add or remove email addresses on your account   3 email addresses

The email address section tops the list, on the righthand side of it click **"Change"**, and on the new screen you can remove any old email addresses and add new ones. Make your business email address the primary email; you will receive a link from LinkedIn you need to click to confirm it is you and the email address will be displayed on your profile.

2: Attracting Traffic to Your Website to Market and Boost Future Sales

The default setting in this section is the phrase "Company Website"; a generic statement that does not inspire action. You need to change this to three clear and inspiring calls to action – phrases that will guide people to take action and, ultimately, send them to your website.

First, decide which three pages of your website you want to send people to and the type of action you want them to take, and then create your messages accordingly. You have up to 30 characters on each call to action line so no waffling here, each directive needs to be concise. For example, you can use:

• Take a look at our Portfolio

• See what our clients say about us

• Click here to book a Workshop

• View our latest products

• Special monthly offers and so on

Here's how to add your website in three easy steps.

Along the top black bar of your LinkedIn screen, click on the word **"Me"**. On the drop down menu click **"View profile"**. Click on the wording **"Contact Info"** which you'll find underneath your profile headline. On the new screen you will see the Website URL box, if you haven't added one yet you will see **"Add a website"**.

Edit contact info   ✕

Profile URL
linkedin.com/in/dawnadlam ↗

Website URL

http://dafreelinkedincoachingcall.gr8.com

Personal
Company
Blog
RSS Feed
Portfolio
✓ Other

Type (Other)

Need LinkedIn help?

Remove website

First, open a new browser bar and type in your website address. Go to the relevant page on your website and copy the page URL from the top of the browser bar. Go back to you LinkedIn profile and paste your webpage link in the Website URL left hand side box. Second, in the right hand side box click the word **"Other"**. Third, in the Type (other) box write your call to action phrase; you have up to 30 characters. Then click the **"Save"** button.

If you only have a one page website then send the person to the same page three times but use three different calls to action. If you have a blog then you can add the blog link, but avoid saying *"Blog"*; add something like " *Follow my regular property updates"*, so people can choose to read what you are talking about.

If you have more than one website, choose first the order you want the websites displayed in and then direct people to different pages on each one. You can change the calls to action and remove the website links as often as you want. It would be good to change once a month especially if you have special offers you want to tell people about. I change mine once a month for each workshop I run as they all have individual booking links.

3: Showing Your Expertise Using Slideshare

Slideshare (www.slideshare.net) is a free online directory where you can, by the click of a button, upload, showcase and share your documents across many social media platforms including LinkedIn.

Alongside the written content on your summary section you can add visual content to your LinkedIn profile. Why not showcase some of your work? When it comes to content, some people respond better to the visual aspect of it rather than to the written one. By adding marketing material in visual form not only will you add colour and interest to your profile you will reach and appeal to a much wider audience: those who prefer visual content; those who prefer written content; and those who would prefer both.

The more people spend time looking at the material on your profile the more they will engage with you which can, in turn, create more opportunities to do business together. As we now speak, I have had nearly one thousand people look at my free " *Guide to LinkedIn in 60 Minutes*" which was uploaded via Slideshare and displayed on my LinkedIn profile.

What marketing material do you have or can you create that will bring your world to life for your audience? Whether you use existing documents you already have on your website or create a series of documents, you should always ask yourself these two crucial questions:

One: Is my content adding value to potential viewers?

Two: Will it spike their interest and generate an action?

If the answer to any of these questions is a no, you should go back and amend your documents before uploading them. It is also very handy to obtain a second opinion, so make sure to ask others for their feedback.

I have a range of documents with tips and hints I share out regularly with LinkedIn users to help them maximise using LinkedIn, which in turn helps me position myself as an expert in my field.

Booster Tip: Always have a call to action at the bottom of each document to help direct the reader take action once they have read it. For example, *"Contact us now for a free website overview"* or *"Special offer this month: half price printing of 500 business cards"* and so on.

Documents you can upload are: Brochures; Case Studies; Testimonials; Photographs; Tips and Hints; Presentations and Infographics. Here's how to do it.

Along the top black bar of your LinkedIn screen click the **"Work"** icon. Go to the bottom right hand side and click the **"Slideshare"** icon. If you go there for the first time, you will be asked for your LinkedIn password and, once inside Slideshare, you are good to go.

So let's now start uploading your documents. Again, it takes only a couple of minutes to upload each one. But what's important to do here is to think about the key searchable words for the title of each document as you upload them. You need to use a compelling title relating to the type of business you are in to maximise your visibility. Here's how.

Click the orange **"Upload"** button on the top right hand side of your Slideshare screen. Choose your document from your desktop or laptop, a PDF file or PowerPoint document is the easiest to upload. Choose the category your information relates to (which helps with keyword search).

Give the document an interesting title. The title of your document is on view on your summary section so grab my attention with a compelling title to make me want to read further and find out more. Then add Tags. Tags are key searchable words and you need to separate each Tag word by a comma. Though you can add up to 20 Tags, aim to have at least five to help get maximum visibility.

Last but not least, add a brief description of the document explaining what relevance it has to the reader, you need to add at least three sentences to help with getting the document noticed. Once your upload has been completed, hover across your image the top righthand side of your Slideshare screen and on the drop down menu click **"My Uploads"**.

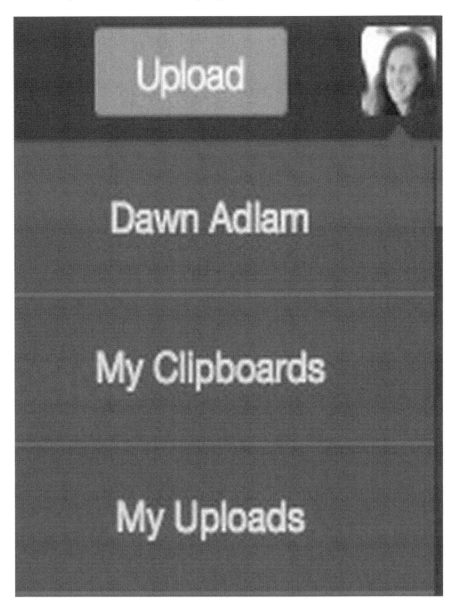

You will then be shown all of your uploaded documents, and as you hover over the latest one you will be asked if you want to add to your LinkedIn profile; click **"Add"**. The documents will be added to the summary section of your LinkedIn profile for people to view and will appear with the latest upload at the bottom of your summary.

Within Slideshare you can click any of the social media **"Share"** buttons located at the bottom of each separate document to push out to other social platforms. How cool and time saving is that? You can amend your documents at any time so you can update them regularly and keep pushing them out to increase the number of followers and grow your audience.

You are now creating a solid database of good content you can share out regularly and quickly with LinkedIn, Facebook and Twitter. As with all marketing and promoting activity, the best results are achieved by sending out short, concise and regular communications.

Another addition to Slideshare is the option of creating a Clipboard. This is a new tool where you can organise research and learn about a new topic by saving and clipping the best content from across Slideshare to view and share at a later date. As you are combing through other people's presentations, on the bottom left of the document you will see the wording **"Clip slide"** and by clipping the slide you can store the it for future use.

You can go anytime to your Clipboard where the individual slides are stored and organise them by author or topic to create a montage of information to share with the wider community. You can choose to make your Clipboard public or private depending upon the type of information you gather.

If the information you are gathering is for your personal use then keep your Clipboard private. To share with others keep your Clipboard public. This is a great way to boost visibility and showcase your expertise on a particular subject or topic.

4: Using YouTube to Increase Your LinkedIn Profile Reach and Visibility

There are two interesting facts about using video as a promotional tool. One, video content increases the understanding of and engagement with your product or services by 74%. Two, YouTube is the second biggest search engine in the world, after Google. What's more, YouTube videos are very easy to upload.

By uploading video content to your LinkedIn profile you can establish serious engagement with your prospective clients and, therefore, increase your *"selling"* capacity. You can use your own videos or alternatively you can search for other interesting video content to upload to your About section on your profile. Don't overload here, just two or three relevant videos would do.

Here's how to upload videos on to your LinkedIn profile:

First, got to www.youtube.com and upload or choose the video you want to use. Once you upload the video, it will have its own URL link, which is found in the browser bar at the top of your screen. Copy this unique link and then go to LinkedIn.

Along the top black bar of your LinkedIn screen, click on the word **"Me"**. On the drop down menu click **"View profile"**. Click the blue pencil on the right hand side of your photo and then scroll down to the About section under which you'll see the word Media. Click the **"Link"** button and paste the unique link beginning with the http:// in the empty **"Paste or type a link to a file or video"** box. Make sure to give a captivating title to your video (avoid the title Company Video) to compel one to view it and add a brief description about its content. Click the blue **"Add"** button and the video will be uploaded automatically onto your About section.

Hire a good video production company who can edit and prepare a professionally finished video. If you prepare it yourself, avoid using shaky home movie style videos, because this is not a professional look and image you want to portray of you or your company.

Create short clips of two or three minute length because people don't have time to spend watching long and boring promotional videos. Your videos should be a snapshot to welcome potential clients or tell an interesting story about you and your company. Some ideas for video content you could post are:

• customer testimonials

• a tour around your premises

• tips & hints to share

• an introduction about your services

• case studies telling a success story or promoting a customer

Supported Media on LinkedIn are:

Video: YouTube, Vimeo, U Stream,

Images: Instagram, Imgur, Flickr,

Rich Media: Prezi, Storify, Slideshare

5: 14 Hidden Gems to Add to Your Profile to Cement Your Professional Standing

There is a lot more you can do to complete and further boost the outreach of your professional LinkedIn profile so it tells your story in as a simple and convincing way as if you were face to face with your client. I always say imagine no one knows you. What would a potential client want to see the first time he or she lands on your LinkedIn profile?

People buy from people, and especially from those they share common grounds with. Give a little insight into you as a person, something people can relate to and may have a common interest in as this can go a long way. It can make your LinkedIn profile, and therefore you, not only more interesting and more human but more approachable and more trusting.

Your Personal Details: By adding your birthday (you don't have to put in the year!) your connections will get an update via the Notifications hub alerting them your upcoming birthday. Popping up brings you into focus and helps with your visibility as well as keeping you in touch with your wider network.

To add your birthday, go to the top black bar of your LinkedIn screen and click on the word **"Me"**. On the drop down menu click **"View profile"**. Click on the blue pencil on the right hand side of the **"More"** button. On the new screen, scroll down to the Contact info section and click on the blue pencil on the right hand side. Scroll to the bottom of the page and add the month and the day you were born and then click the blue **"Save"** button.

Contact info

Profile URL, Websites, Phone, Email, Twitter, Instant Messenger, Birthday, WeChat ID

This works both ways. I have generated new business by wishing happy birthday to one of my connections, who later on replied to thank me and said she had been thinking of getting some LinkedIn training and asked if I could give her a call. I did and a deal followed!

Below are additional sections you can add to your LinkedIn profile to generate more interest. These sections are found on your LinkedIn profile, to the right hand side of your profile. Do you volunteer for good causes? Can you speak another language? Do you belong to any professional organisations? Fill out the ones that are relevant to you and your career. Here's how to add them.

Along the top black bar of your LinkedIn screen, click on the word **"Me"**. On the drop down menu click **"View profile"**. On the far right hand side of the page, click the white arrow on the blue **"Add profile section"** button and a drop down menu will appear.

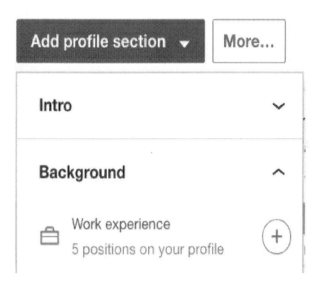

When you click the black facing down arrow on the side of each subsection you'll see the options available; then by clicking on the plus sign in a circle next to each section you can add more details accordingly.

Background: List your Work experience history, add your Education (you get 11 x more views by adding your school) and highlight your volunteering activities. Click on the **"+"** icon to add the details you want on display and then click the blue **"Save"** button.

Education: Add your School or College. Click on the **"+"** icon to add the details you want on display and then click the blue **"Save"** button.

Volunteering: Add the Charities, Causes you support. Click on the **"+"** icon to add the details you want on display and then click the blue **"Save"** button.

Skills: Add your skills to showcase your strengths as a professional. All you need to do is click on the **"+"** icon to add the details you want on display and then click the blue **"Save"** button.

Accomplishments: In this area there are nine options you can choose from.

Publications – list your published work as it helps improve your visibility sevenfold.

Certifications – LinkedIn members with a certification get five times more profile views.

Courses – list coursework from previous or current education.

Projects – add projects to demonstrate and showcase your experience.

Honors & Awards – feature the recognition you've earned, it's where you can blow your own trumpet!

Test Scores – if you have excelled in any exams go ahead and list your score here.

Languages – another place to showcase your ability for overseas opportunities.

Organisations – Show your involvement with communities that are important to you.

All of these sections help build up your personality and image and cement your position in the marketplace.

6: How to Put the "WOW" Factor into Your LinkedIn Profile with a Background Photo

The LinkedIn Background Photograph is a cool feature where you can add further spark and interest on your profile. This image sits behind your headline and your personal photograph and can produce a wow factor when people view your profile.

Think about adding an image that represents a theme of your business rather than its logo. You don't want to sell or shout about your brand as soon as someone lands on your profile (remember, people are not interested in buying from you at this stage). You need to generate interest first.

The banner could be a graduated colour related to your brand, a logo or a montage of images related to your services. The image needs to be a JPEG, GIF or PNG and smaller than 8MB and resolutions pixel dimensions between 1584 x 396. Here's how to add this image.

Along the top black bar of your LinkedIn screen, click on the word **"Me"**. On the drop down menu click **"View profile"**. Click the blue pencil on the right hand side of your profile, and in the new screen, above your photo, click the background image pencil to upload the background image – it's that simple! Click the blue **"Save"** button to save the changes.

You can use Canva, www.canva.com, to create your own banner or search www.freelinkedinbackgroundimages.com for more banner ideas.

Congratulations, your LinkedIn profile is now complete! You have the strongest and most effective LinkedIn profile and are now ready to put your sales and marketing strategy together.

This is where it now gets interesting and you can make a real headway in getting noticed and generating new clients. Take a well-deserved break, put the kettle on, flex the fingers and get ready for the next stage on your LinkedIn journey.

Part II
LinkedIn Marketing For LinkedIn Success

3

Finding the Right Contacts to Reach Key Decision Makers

Do you have a LinkedIn profile but not many connections and not much activity going on? If you have, you can change all that. You do so by committing to a regular LinkedIn activity, which is about creating a prospecting strategy that is proactive rather than reactive. It is a process of searching for, connecting and communicating with and, eventually, generating and helping new clients.

Think about how you built your existing customer base. Did you sit waiting for new clients and sales to come to you or did you go out and get them? It's the same with LinkedIn. By adding new people and growing your network over time, you will create a powerful database of connections who, by following your activity on LinkedIn, will have the chance to interact and do business with you.

Let's start with the crucial sales and marketing question: who are the people you are able to help? In other words, identify your ideal customer. With that in mind, you can then work out where and how you find and target your ideal customer within LinkedIn, meaning you are now ready to start the process of sales and marketing.

You can locate a potential client by searching through People; Companies; or Groups. The search facility is located along the top of the black bar on the left of your LinkedIn screen. In order to filter the type of search you want to do, click on the looking glass icon and a new screen will appear. There are three types of searches you should focus on to get results:

One: you can search for individual people by their name by clicking the **"People"** option. In this example, I typed Pardip Singhota in the search bar, and a drop down menu appears with only one result showing as she is a 1st line connection.

Two: you can search for a company by name via the **"Companies"** option. Click the search icon on the top left hand side of the black bar and on the drop down menu click **"Companies"**. Type the name of the company you would like to view in the search bar and on the drop down list click on the company page . Click the **"Follow"** button to see all their updates and posts.

Three: you can search for groups via the **"Groups"** option. Click the search icon on the top left hand side of the black bar and on the drop down menu click **"Groups"**. Groups are small, medium or large hubs of people within LinkedIn where your ideal prospects are bound to be. It could be a local business or an industry specific group.

For example, if you are in the property sector and are based in the UK, there is a large UK Commercial Property group which would be highly beneficial to join and be active in. Type UK Commercial Property Group in the search bar and a list will appear where you'll find and can join the above group.

Q UK Commercial Property

Q See all results for "uk commercial property"

UK COMMERCIAL PROPERTY
Group

UK Commercial Property Investment Deals
Group

Once you became a member of a group, you can search through its members to identify new contacts you want to make and send them a direct message. You can also become an influencer within the group, which will seriously boost your professional standing. See Chapter 10 on how to use successfully the massive potential of LinkedIn groups.

These three search methods are the basic starting points of using LinkedIn to track down the right prospects for you. Can you see now how important identifying the type of person you can help is?

Once you have mastered these three search options, the next step is to start building on this by creating a LinkedIn user strategy specific to you and your business goals. Having a clear plan to achieve these goals makes the difference between being reactive, which is waiting for people to come to you; and proactive, which is you going out there and finding them.

I will show you three highly productive ways on how to find new clients and start generating new business. It comes down to committing to regular activity to raise your profile and in return your visibility.

You don't want to be the best kept secret on LinkedIn; instead, you want as much exposure as possible to stand out from the crowd and grow your contact database organically and with the right type of connections. Let's make a start!

How to Hone Your LinkedIn Search Skills to

Uncover a Lucrative Sales Pipeline

It's time to sharpen your search skill level in more detail by using a more detailed approach to using the search facility. With the tips I am about to share you can hone your search and start creating a devastatingly powerful prospecting list from which you can drill down to find the people you can help and do business with.

Once you identify and create a list of potential clients you move on crafting a message to make the right approach. LinkedIn is a great tool for achieving this purpose, but don't go straight into sales mode before you have even spoken to a prospect, because, as you know, no one likes to be sold to. Here's what you need to do.

Along the top black bar of your LinkedIn screen, click on the looking glass in the search bar top left of your screen. You will be taken to a new screen where you'll see many types of advanced searches to choose from.

Depending upon the information you already have you can search for: people by name; company by name; a keyword, a job title, location and type of industry.

For example, let's say you would like to search for and find a HR person locally (someone you don't yet know but would like to get to know). Using this example, I typed **HR Coventry** into the search bar narrowing down the location before executing the search.

Q HR Coventry

Top People

You can further filter the search using the Connections section, under which you tick the most relevant to your search criteria based on:

• 1st Connections – people you are already connected to

• 2nd Connections – people your 1st connections are connected to

• 3rd + Everyone else – third degree connections in the chain of connectivity (this option has the least results as the trail gets colder when there are more people involved in the chain)

Connections ▼

☐ 1st

☐ 2nd

☐ 3rd+

I selected my 2nd line connections – people I am not connected to on

LinkedIn. Click the blue **"Apply"** button. The next step is to add the keyword in the title section; I typed HR.

Keywords ⌃

First name

Last name

Title

HR

I then selected the geographical location of Coventry. Specify where you want to start your search – locally or further afield in a particular city. With 23 million LinkedIn members in the UK, this would be too wide a search so you filter the search to a geographical area.

Locations

 Coventry, United Kingdom

Next I selected the industry Human Resources. You can include a company type too if you know where the connection currently works.

Alternatively you could include a past Company to search for. Using LinkedIn as a real time prospecting list building tool, the obvious choice would be selecting the person's current role at the moment you search – that is how you get through to the relevant decision makers.

On each step of selection process you are honing your search and every time you select an option LinkedIn will filter until you are left with a list, in this case it is showing 94 results of people with HR in their title based on my 2nd line connections in Coventry. Voila! A prospect list has appeared!

Start working through the list identifying who you would like to connect with and start the conversation. Click on their profile and from here click the blue **"Connect"** button.

Before sending the request, do add a personalised message; research shows people are much more likely to accept your connection request if sent with a personal message. Click the blue **"Connect"** button and on the new screen click **"Add a note"** wording; write a short message and click the blue **"Send now"** button.

Spend some time working out the type of new connections you would like to add to your network based on the search filters and create a set of prospect lists. Also, create a series of connection messages that will help you get through to the persons you want to connect with, rather than send them a dreaded sales pitch.

I have two prospects lists that I work through regularly – Sales Training, and Sales Director whom I know I can help by training their sales teams on how to use LinkedIn. Each week I spend time researching each person, making a connection request and start prospecting with conversations. Note that I use the singular "sales director", not "sales directors" when searching. Other search phrases to use are:

• NOT searches: To exclude a particular term, type that term with an uppercase NOT immediately before it. For example, type "programmer NOT manager".

• OR searches: To see results that include one or more terms in a list, separate the terms with an uppercase OR. For example, type "sales OR marketing".

• AND searches: To get results that include two or more terms in a list, you can use the uppercase word AND as a separator. For example, type "manager AND director".

Another great method of using the search facility is to communicate with your 1st line connections, the people you already know or someone you accepted into your network but have never spoken to – it's good practice to message them and re-establish some rapport together. Here's an example.

Search for property developers you are already connected to, click the looking glass icon top left of your LinkedIn screen. Type "Property Developer" Birmingham and then select 1st line connections.

Booster Tip: If you want to search a keyword phrase link the words together using speech marks, otherwise LinkedIn will search both words independently and this will make the search far too wide.

The search will show you a list of property developers who you are already connected to. If you spot connections in the list you have never spoken to, now is the time to start a conversation with them. You can say, for example:

"Hi John

We are connected on LinkedIn but I realise we have never actually spoken. Are you available next week to schedule a call together so I can find out more about you and look at working together?

Kind regards

Booster Tip: It is worth noting you only have a percentage of searches each month on the basic version of LinkedIn so always type a location to keep the search to a minimum. Your search volume is reset on the first of every month.

You can repeat this whole exercise for connections you don't know, your 2nd line connections, click 2nd line instead of 1st line connections and you have a prospect list of people you don't know.

Booster Tip: When looking a LinkedIn member's profile, take a look on the right hand side of your screen – the People Also Viewed list. LinkedIn suggest other types of people based on the profile you are looking at which is a great way to prospect for similar new connections.

Leveraging Your LinkedIn Connections for Leads and Ideal Clients

There are two more ways to search for prospects.

First, you look through the connections of your connections to spot who they know who may be good introductions for you. You can search through one of your 1st line connection's contacts (I am assuming you already know your 1st line connection) and then ask him or her for introductions to people in their network.

Booster Tip: Located underneath your headline (and everyone else's headline) there is the Connections component. Here you can search through your 1st line connections to find out who they know who would be ideal introductions for you.

Go to one of your 1st line connection's profile and click on the **"connections"** text. A list will appear showing Shared connections and all connections. Scroll through and when you identify someone you would like to be connected to, ask your 1st line connection to introduce you.

Here's how to ask and make an introduction.

Go to one of your 1st line connection's profile and click on the **"connections"** text. A list will appear showing both shared connections and all connections. Click **"Connections"** and on the drop down menu filter first your search by 2nd or 3rd line connections depending on your preference. Click the blue **"Apply"** button.

Scroll through and when you identify someone you would like to be connected to, ask your 1st line connection to introduce you. Here's how to ask and make an introduction.

Go to the profile of one of your 1st line connections (whom you know well), search through their connections and identify someone you would like an introduction to.

Along the top black bar of the LinkedIn screen click the **"Messaging"** icon. Once inside the Messaging section click on the blue square icon to start a new message.

Messaging

Type the name of your 1st line connection, write the message asking for an introduction to connect and click **"Send"**.

Messaging	🖉	New message
Q Search messages	⇌	Type a name or multiple names...

If someone asks you to do the same, follow the instructions above, but make sure to add the name of the person you want to connect them to.

Write the personal message of introduction as to how it could potentially be of benefit to each other to have a conversation together and click **"Send"**.

"Hi Pardip

Can I introduce you to Matt Wallis please; he is looking to make contact with a local HR consultant so I suggested it would be worth a conversation together.

Let me know how you get on.

Regards

Remember, if you are not connected to a person you cannot see their connections, only the ones you are both connected to. So if you don't want your competitors to see who you are connected to, don't connect to them!

There's also a group feature to message people collectively. Along the top black bar of the LinkedIn screen click the **"Messaging"** icon. Click on the **"People"** icon and start typing in the participants names. Name the list (optional), click **"Next"** and send the message.

The second way to search for prospects is from the mutual connections list. Go to a 2nd line connection's profile, underneath their headline, you will see Highlights: the number of mutual connections. For example, below I have 100 mutual connections and can ask any of them to introduce me.

Highlights

100 mutual connections
You and Paulin Prifti both know Reuben Miller MRICS MSc PG Dip FNAEA CPEA, Justine Rixon, and 98 others

This is a much warmer way of connecting, but please don't jump into selling mode at this stage. Keep it simple and make the approach asking if your 1st line connection would be willing to make the introduction. Also, add that you would be happy to return the favour anytime.

"Hi Pardip

I see you are connected to Debbie Pettingill, and I am looking for a good local recruitment agency. Would you introduce us, please?

Happy to return the favour.

Your 1st line connection can then send an email via LinkedIn and add you both onto the email. To do this, click on the **"Messaging"** icon in the top black bar of the LinkedIn screen.

Once inside the email section, click the blue square icon to compose the message and send to both connections with a personal message introducing the two of them. But remember that building a good and solid database of connections is not about quantity, it is about the quality of your network.

Good 1st line connections are the link to your 2nd line connections. You should make it a priority to connect to them because it is where the real and untapped value is to be found.

Making a few generic connections randomly will grow your database of connections, but compare that to a structured approach of using the advanced search alongside asking for personal introductions means you can keep a steady pipeline of new people to speak to. One new connection a day would be potentially 20 people a month to arrange calls and speak too, easily achievable if planned and actioned daily.

How to Expand Your LinkedIn Network Fast with Free Connections

LinkedIn offer you the option to connect to people they think you might know and you don't need to know their email addresses in order to connect. This is a good way to prospect and build your network easily and quickly. But bear in mind that once your connection request is accepted, you must continue the dialogue with the new connection by arranging a call or a meeting. The fortune is always in the follow up; this will give you the edge over your competition because most people accept the connection request and then do nothing else. That's a wasted opportunity. You will find these opportunities to connect in three different places.

One: On the LinkedIn Home page, which is located along the top back bar of your LinkedIn screen next to My Network.

Click the word **"Home"**. Once inside the Home Page there is a continual stream of updates and information that LinkedIn users are sharing with their network, this is the social side, the marketing hub of LinkedIn. Within the stream of information you will see new connections that your 1st line contacts are talking about and promoting, you can click onto these new profiles and ask to connect in the usual way.

Always personalise the connection request message, and to build your network you need a mix of people you know along with new people that you don't know yet. Two a day would give you ten new connections opportunities a week. Bringing new connections into your network is a good organic way to grow your database. Remember though; when the person accepts your request always follow up with him or her.

Two: The pending invitations to connect box. Along the top black bar of your LinkedIn screen, next to the Home icon, click on **"My Network"**. On the new screen you will see your outstanding invitations to connect.

Click the **"Manage"** wording on the right hand side and the list of people will appear. You now have three options.

First, click on the blue **"Accept"** button to add the person to your network and start a conversation with them. Second, click **"Ignore"** if you do not want to accept the request (no one can see you refuse a connection request).

Third, reply before accepting their connection request by clicking the blue **"Message"** wording. When it comes to the third option you want to know the reason why he or she wants to connect to you – you may not know them.

To do this, click on the blue **"Message"** text underneath their photograph. You will now be taken to your email section where you can send a message and ask them how you can help them or ask why they want to connect, rather than just ignore them. Type out your message, as the one below, and click **"Send"**.

"Hi Damian

Many thanks for offering to connect. How can I help you?

I look forward to hearing from you.

Regards

I treat each new request as a new business opportunity. I had a request from a lady based miles away in Manchester whom I didn't know. I replied thanking her for reaching out and asked how I could help her. She replied saying that since they were moving to Birmingham she wanted to speak to me about LinkedIn training. I could easily have missed this opportunity if I hadn't asked the question or, worse, ignored the request.

Three: People you may know. Within My network section underneath the invitation requests there is another option for new connections.

It is under the heading More suggestions for you section, and it includes People, Groups, Pages and Hashtags. As above, use it to make new connection and grow your network.

More suggestions for you

People	Groups	Pages	Hashtags

This section provides a valuable list of 2nd line connections and as with all previous 2nd line connections click on the blue **"Connect"** button to connect. You don't need their email address to ask to connect, but please include a personalised message.

LinkedIn members are more likely to connect with a personal message. Write a simple personal message such as the one following and click the blue **"Send invitation"** button and it's done.

Not all the invitations to connect would bring in a response; the majority would definitely do so, though some may take more time than others. Be patient and it'll happen.

"Hi Pat

Many thanks for visiting our group this morning. I would like to connect on LinkedIn, please.

I look forward to hearing from you.

Regards

These random connections are *colder* prospects without a warm introduction but the same process applies when receiving a new connection: engage with them and always, always follow up if they accept your request.

LinkedIn is quite intuitive so, for example, if you connect to Demolition people regularly, LinkedIn will suggest other Demolition people you may know, all making life a little simpler!

Keep reading for the best way to prospect using the Company Pages within LinkedIn – I think you will love this, I do!

Maximising Company Pages to Connect to Key People in Your Target Market

I mentioned earlier in this Chapter that you can follow company pages to see company activity, job advertising and updates but there is an even better use for company pages. Just by the click of a button you can see all the employees that are associated with the company who are on LinkedIn.

Let me show you how. Along the top black bar of your LinkedIn screen click on the search bar. On the new screen type the name of the company page you want to look at. In this example I have chosen Coca-Cola.

A list of options will appear. Click the Coca-Cola company page and you will be taken to its LinkedIn page. When looking at the company page, on the right hand side of the screen you can see a list of all the employees who are on LinkedIn and the connections you have in common.

You'll find Coca-Cola have over 70,000 employees worldwide on LinkedIn. This is too wide a range; you need to specify the search. Click the blue **"See all** 70,000 **employees"** text and on a new screen a list of employees will appear, you can then filter them by country and geographical area.

This is a quick and easy method to search for people within a particular company and in my opinion one of LinkedIn's hidden gems which you now know how to use. But don't forget to follow the process as laid out above when you find your ideal person; click the blue **"Connect"** button on their profile and then write a personalised message.

If the person is a 3rd line connection, you can still connect without needing to pay for the premium version of LinkedIn. Simply go to that connection's profile and on the right hand side of the blue **"Message"** button click on the box with the three dots and on the drop down message click **"Connect"**. How cool is that? Again always include a personal message when connecting. Happy prospecting!

But we haven't quite finished yet; keep reading for more ways to prospect successfully on LinkedIn.

Two More Ways to Maximise the LinkedIn Search Features

Let me share two more methods of searching and prospecting that link together with LinkedIn to enhance your activity.

One: Take a look at RecruitEm where you can use Google to search for profiles on LinkedIn: https://recruitin.net/. The benefits to using this option are as follows.

• Generate more than 100 results

• Find out of your network connections for a wider outreach of people to connect to

• Search by education or employer

• No registration needed

• It's free

It is really simple to use and includes an X-Ray search of the Country, Location and words to include, Job Title, Keywords to exclude, Education and Current Employer. For example, I am looking to reach out to local accountants in Coventry, so I type "accountant" in the keyword box, "United Kingdom" in the Country box and "Coventry" in the Location box. Once filled in, go and click the green **"Find the right people on LinkedIn"** button.

Find the right people on LinkedIn

A search will appear, click on the green **"Open in Google"** button and your prospecting list of accountants in Coventry will appear.

Copy, save or open the search string in Google and find the right candidates

http://www.google.com/search?q=+"accountant"+"Coventry" -intitle:"profiles" -inurl:"dir/

⟨╱ Copy URL   **⚲ Save Search**   **☐ Open in Google**

Follow the same process as above, click on each profile and click the blue **"Connect"** button to send them a personalised message to connect. Yes it really is that easy. To save time you can save your search if you wanted to dip into it regularly. Click the middle orange **"Save Search"** button, which you will find it in the blue box on the top right hand side of your LinkedIn screen.

Making the same search regularly?

Save it, then find it here!

Another benefit is searching Twitter too. Click on the **"Twitter"** wording on the far right hand side of your screen, fill the search boxes with the country and keywords you want to include or exclude and then click the green **"Find the right people on Twitter"** button.

Easily use Google to search profiles on Twitter

City or Country ⦾

> E.g. New York or London

Skills (keywords) to include ⦾

> E.g. PHP, Ruby, Linux

Skills (keywords) to exclude ⦾

> E.g. Illustrator

> Find the right people on Twitter

You can then follow people and companies and when they follow you back you will get a notification, send a direct message to them and start a conversation together. Another simple form of prospecting you might not have thought of using.

Two: Using the Advanced Google search facility: https://www.google.co.uk/advanced_search. From here you can scan LinkedIn profiles and create a prospect list through Google. Here's how this works.

Click on the link above and you will be taken to the Advanced Search Google Page. Fill in the first section which is all about Keywords (this goes back to the importance of having good searchable words in your headline). For example, I search for sales and marketing directors (use singular wording) in Birmingham but nothing to do with jobs relating to these keywords.

Find pages with...

all these words:	sales director
this exact word or phrase:	"sales and marketing director"
any of these words:	birmingham
none of these words:	jobs

Continue to narrow the search in the second set of boxes below and in the site or domain box type **"linkedin.com"**.

Then narrow your results by...

language:	any language
region:	any region
last update:	anytime
site or domain:	linkedin.com

Click the blue **"Advanced Search"** button to generate a list of LinkedIn profiles that match these criteria. Take some time to hone the keywords to use and words you don't want to include.

It will take a little trial and error to get the exact results but I'm sure this will help you create a relevant prospect list to work through. The results of this particular search example generated 25,300 results!

The keywords entered are highlighted in bold. Follow the same connection process as already discussed, from the person's profile on LinkedIn click the blue **"Connect"** button and personalise the connection message.

In a nutshell, this Chapter will help you build the cornerstone strategy you can commit to and which, over time, will generate you new business opportunities. Start by identifying the decision makers you want to speak to. It's helpful to do some research outside of LinkedIn first, and then come back to LinkedIn and use either its search box facility or LinkedIn Company Pages and LinkedIn Groups to find them and then approach and connect to them.

Once connected to a person, engage with them and start a conversation. Some people will buy your services, some won't. Most sales are generated from starting a good working relationship together because people buy from people.

As soon as you make a brand new connection decide what happens next in your sales cycle; organise a call, a skype session or arrange a meeting. Because just connecting with someone and creating no further interaction is not going to generate new business.

Be proactive and go and get new clients; what's the worst that can happen? You may get no response initially, but by keeping your visibility going with LinkedIn articles and updates you'll find that people will buy from you further down the road.

Okay, we're just getting started. In the next chapter we will look at ways to widen your influence further and continue with creating a prospect list.

4

Tracking Your LinkedIn Connections

How to Identify Valuable Connections and Build Business Relationships

I was speaking to someone recently who told me they had a large network of connections but didn't know who half of them were. This is not uncommon. But is it too late to contact people after you have had them in your network for a while? It isn't. You can re-engage with your connections and move them closer towards becoming potential clients. Let's find out first who you are already connected to but may have never spoken to.

Along the top black bar of your LinkedIn screen click on **"My Network"**. On the new screen, click **"Connections"** in the top left hand side box.

Manage my network

Connections   6,719

Teammates

You will now see the list of all your connections on LinkedIn. In short, the Connections hub comprises of all your 1st line connections in one place – it is your LinkedIn filing cabinet of connections from A to Z. Isn't it useful to know you have all your LinkedIn connections in one place?

6,719 Connections

Sort by: Recently added ▼

Q Search by name   Search with filters

Your 1st line connections are displayed in chronological order. You can filter them choosing either First name or Last name by clicking the arrow next to the **"Recently added"** text. You can also search by typing in the search box on the right hand side.

Set yourself the task of working through your existing connections to identifying potential clients to speak to. When you come across a connection you don't know yet whom you would like to know, you can send them a direct message. Here's what you need to do.

As you are going through the list of your connections, hover over the connection you want to send a message to and click the blue **"Message"** icon on the right hand side. Craft a personal message that would encourage people to want to speak to you, but be careful not to go into selling mode at this stage, and once you have typed your message click the blue **"Send"** button on the bottom right hand side.

Here are a couple of email examples you can use to re-engage with your existing network of connections:

"Hi Charles, I realize we are first line connections but have never actually spoken.

When would be a good time to give you a call to see how we might help each other? Are you around next Tuesday?

Kind regards

"Hi Charles, we are first line connections on LinkedIn but have never actually spoken.

I am looking to build some local alliances and I would be interested in finding out more about you and how we might work together. Are you open for a call together next week?

Kind regards

Test and measure responses and select the ones that generate a response – keep using them to arrange calls and meetings in your diary. Believe me, you will have potential clients hiding in your network, start re communicating with them and you could unlock a massive pipeline for your business.

How to Open the Door to New LinkedIn Connections Using No Email Address

Here is one of the questions I get asked most often, *"How do you add a new LinkedIn connection without knowing the email address of the person you want to connect to?"*

Using LinkedIn successfully and profitably is about growing your LinkedIn network not only with connections you already know but also with connections you don't yet know but would like to. The simplest way to do this when looking at the profile of a 2nd line connection you want to reach out to is to click the blue **"Connect"** button.

On the new screen you now have two options; click the blue **"Send now"** button or **"Add a note"** button. Always click **"Add a note"** and remember to personalise the message. Aside not leaving people guessing why you want to connect, LinkedIn members are most likely to accept invitations that include a personal note. Wouldn't you accept such invitation?

The recipient will be able to read your note before they accept or ignore your request, so be honest and say the reason why you want to connect or mention something you have in common with them. Keep the message brief at this stage; once you are connected you can then expand the conversation.

I think you'll agree that this is a really simple way to grow your LinkedIn network in a professional and strategic way. The crucial part is knowing what to do once you have acquired a new connection, because connecting on LinkedIn and then taking no further action is a pure waste of time.

You need to make it a priority to engage and communicate with a new connection. Specify first where do they fit into your network – a new supplier, a referral giver or a potential new client – and then get in touch.

Whatever your next step is, please don't jump in and "sell" your services. At the very least, begin by asking how you can help and if they are open for a conversation. Why not arrange a call together or meet for coffee? You could be dealing with your next biggest customer or supplier, but if you don't start building a relationship I guarantee they will turn elsewhere!

You now have a plan to make the most of your existing and new connections and a way forward to keep a track of all your new connections. Keep reading to find out the most effective approach you can use to get results after you have added a new LinkedIn connection.

5

How to Communicate Directly and Effectively on LinkedIn to Connect to a Deeper Level with Anyone Who Matters to You and Your Business

As a busy professional, you need to control the flow of information you receive from LinkedIn to make it efficient and effective in the long run. It will save you time and also keep the communication channels flowing smoothly.

It may take you a couple of hours to work through LinkedIn's Privacy and Settings hub; it is worth the effort though as it will be extremely useful to control the stream of incoming and outgoing information to best suit you. It is easy to change your LinkedIn profile settings to facilitate this. Here's how.

Along the top black bar of your LinkedIn screen, click on the word **"Me"** and on the drop down menu click **"Settings & Privacy"**. Once you are in the Settings & Privacy hub you have three sections to go through and set up: Account; Privacy; and Communications.

I will cover each of these sections below and although for the most part they are self-explanatory, some clarification will help you make the right decision.

Optimising Your Account Settings

In the Account Settings you will find the following options: Login and security; Site preferences; Subscriptions and payments; Partners and services and lastly Account management.

Login and security: From here you can change, add or remove any of the basic elements of your LinkedIn profile including:

Email address – always use your work email address as primary instead of a personal one to give that professional impression.

Phone numbers – add a second telephone number in case you have trouble signing in.

Change password – choose a unique password that is case sensitive and at least six characters (you'll need to enter your current password to make any changes).

Where you're signed in – you can see your last three active sessions and can sign out of them and any Third Party applications which will save you time.

Two-step Verification – you should go for enhanced account security, especially if other people have access to your laptop or devices. By turning on the two-step verification process you'll be signed out and required to enter a verification code when using new devices or mobile applications.

Site preferences: From here you can control communication; what you have on display and can see on display including:

Language – choose the language you are most comfortable using on LinkedIn.

Auto-play videos – choose if you want the videos in your home page feed to automatically play or not.

Showing profile photos – chose whether to show or to hide profile photos of other members: Everyone; Your Network; Your Connections; or No one. The best option would be to go for Everyone.

Feed preferences – follow people to see their posts related to your field.

Name, location and industry – chose how your name and how your other profile fields appear to other members.

Subscriptions and payments: From here you can take a look at the premium options available and the benefits including:

Upgrade for Free – take a look at the options available, you will need to enter payment details for a month's trial.

View Purchase history – see all your previous purchases and transactions on LinkedIn.

Partners and Services: From this section you can change, add or remove any of the third party services you have associated with your LinkedIn account. This is your list of authorised external partner applications you have granted access to your LinkedIn profile enabling you to show examples of your work.

Permitted services – view the services you have authorised and also manage date sharing.

Twitter settings – add another Twitter account (you can have up to two accounts) and click to display your Twitter account on your LinkedIn profile.

Microsoft – view Microsoft accounts you have connected to your LinkedIn account. You can, in this way, control which Microsoft accounts you grant access to your LinkedIn data.

Account management: From here you can do the following:

Merge your LinkedIn accounts – transfer connections from a duplicate account, then close it.

Closing your LinkedIn account – learn about your options and close your account if you wish.

If you want to make any changes to any of the above, first go to the Settings & Privacy hub. Click on the word **"Change"** on the right hand side of your screen and amend each section as necessary.

Controlling Your Privacy Settings

In the Privacy Settings you can choose the following options: Profile and network information; How others see your LinkedIn activity; How LinkedIn uses your data; Job seeking preferences; and Blocking and hiding.

Profile and network information: From here you can pull the strings from behind the scenes of your profile in more detail including:

Edit your public profile – choose how your profile appears in search engines; visible to one or visible to everyone.

Who can see your email address – choose from only you, 1st line connections, 1st and 2nd line connections or everyone on LinkedIn. I have mine set to 1st line connections as I am happy for them to see my contact details.

Who can see your connections – it is either you or all your connections. LinkedIn is an open forum so you should have all your connections on view. I don't have any of my competitors in my network who can see my connections. With any of my trusted connections I know well I am happy to make new introductions to other people in my network if it would benefit them.

Viewers of this profile also viewed – this feature makes suggestions of similar LinkedIn profiles based on your previous profile search history which can help highlighting potential new connections for you.

Who can see your last name – choose how you want to surname to appear –

in full or not. I have my surname set to full for maximum visibility.

Representing your organisation and interests – choose if you want LinkedIn to mention you with content about your employers or other content you publicly expressed and interest in.

Profile visibility off LinkedIn – choose how your profile appears via partners' and other permitted services such as Microsoft Outlook.

Microsoft Word – choose if you would like to have your LinkedIn profile work experience description be displayed in Resume Assistant.

How others see your LinkedIn activity: From here you can monitor your visibility within LinkedIn including:

Profile viewing options – choose how visible you prefer to be: fully visible; partially visible; or anonymous. I am always on fully visible to maximise visibility.

Manage active status – choose who can see when you are on LinkedIn: you connections only, all LinkedIn members or no one. I have mine set to all LinkedIn members to help me get extra visibility.

Sharing profile edits – choose whether your network is notified about changes to your profile, recommendations you make or companies you follow. Click yes and start gettting noticed on LinkedIn!

Notifying connections when you're in the news – this is about letting your connections and followers know when you are mentioned in an article or blog post. For that extra visibility, click yes!

Mentions by others – choose whether other members can mention you. I have clicked Yes for maximum impact.

How LinkedIn uses your data: From here you can control how LinkedIn uses your data including:

Manage your data and activity – review the data you have provided and make changes if you want to.

Manage who can discover your profile from your email address – choose who can discover your profile if they are not connected to you but have your email address; everyone, 2nd line connections or no one.

Manage who can discover your profile from your phone number – choose who can discover your profile if they have your phone number; everyone, 2nd line connections or no one.

Sync contacts – manage or sync contacts to connect with people you know directly from your address book.

Sync calendar – manage or sync your calendar to get timely updates about who you will be meeting with.

Salary data on LinkedIn – see and delete your salary data.

Search history – your seach history is only visible to you, clear all previous searches performed on LinkedIn.

Social, economic and workplace research – choose whether LinkedIn can make some of your data available to trusted services for policy and academic research.

Job seeking preferences: From here you can make yourself visible to recruiters using the following options.

Let recruiters know you're open to opportunities – share that you are open an appear in recruiter searches matching your career interests.

Sharing your profile when you click apply – choose if you want to share your full profile with the job poster when you are taken off LinkedIn after clicking apply.

Stored job applicant accounts – manage which third party job applicant accounts are stored on LinkedIn.

Saving job application answers – choose if you would like LinkedIn to sabe the information you enter into job applications.

Blocking and hiding: This is where you pull the strings behind the scenes on how you communicate with your followers and public updates including:

Followers – choose who can follow you and all see your public updates on LinkedIn; everyone or just your followers. For more visibility click everyone.

Blocking – you can report or block someone if they are sending inappropriate material. I have never had reason to do this in all the years I have been using LinkedIn. But, if you need to do this, go to that person's LinkedIn profile and click on the circle with the three dots on the right hand side. On the drop down menu that appears select **"Report / Block"**.

Unfollowed – see who you have unfollowed (content that is hidden from view) and there is the option to follow back if you change your mind.

Sharpening Your Marketing Preferences

In the Ads Settings you have the following options: General advertising preferences, Data collected on LinkedIn and Third Party data.

Ads: From here you can check your advertising preferences to maximise your interests and data collection including:

General advertising preferences

Insights on websites you visited – see more relevant promoted jobs and ads based on website visit insights.

Ads beyond LinkedIn – see more relevant promoted jobs and ads on websites and apps off LinkedIn.

Profile data for ad personalization – control how certain ads appear to you.

Data collected on LinkedIn

Interest categories – see more relevant promoted jobs and ads based on your and similar members' activity on LinkedIn.

Connections – see more relevant promoted jobs and ads based on your connections.

Location – see more relevant promoted jobs and ads based on your post code or city.

Demographics – see more relevant ads based on your demographic data.

Companies you follow – see more relevant promoted jobs and ads based on companie you follow.

Groups – see more relevant promoted jobs and ads based on groups you joined.

Education – see more relevant promoted jobs and ads based on your education.

Job information – see more relevant promoted jobs and ads based on your job information.

Third Party data

Interactions with businesses – see more relevant promoted jobs and ads based on information or consent given to businesses.

Ad-related actions – see more relevant promoted jobs and ads based on actions you took on ads.

Ok, we are now ready to move on to the last section, the Communication Settings.

Tweaking Your Communications Settings

There are four parts to this section: Channels; Preferences; Groups; and LinkedIn messages. From here you can control the flow of communication as follows.

Channels

Notifications on LinkedIn – manage the alerts you receive in the notifications tab.

Email frequency – choose what type of emails you wish to receive from LinkedIn and you can also set detailed frequency preferences from here too.

Preferences

Who can send you invitations – choose who can send you invitation to connect

Messages from members and partners – let LinkedIn know what type of messages you would prefer to receive.

Read receipts and typing indicators – choose whether or not you want to send and receive read receipts for your messages.

Message reply suggestions – choose if you want to see recommended replies when responding to a message.

Groups: From here you can show how open you are to group requests including:

Group invitations – choose whether you want to receive invitations to join groups.

LinkedIn Messages: It is here you can be open to feedback surveys or market research including:

Participate in research – participate or not in market research studies. Participation is 100% voluntary and personal information is not revealed.

If you want to make any changes to any of the above, first go to the Privacy and Settings hub. Click on the word **"Change"** on the right hand side of your screen and amend each section as necessary.

Next, you'll learn how to turn connections into those clients and who are willing to pay for what you offer. Most people ignore or don't bother with this part of marketing strategy; use it to your advantage and the sky would be the limit.

6

The Secret of Turning Your Ideal Prospects into Meetings and Paying Customers

If LinkedIn's untapped potential is used the right way it can be a tremendously effective sales generation tool and propel your business way ahead of your competition. To make this happen, you need to get started with three crucial questions:

One: what does your sales pipeline look like? In other words, how many steps does it take to make a new sale?

Two: what approach and methods do you have in place to generating new customers?

Three: what are the underlying principles of your sales process?

It is unlikely you will go from having a connection request accepted to striking a deal and making a sale straight away. Every new connection you make, and therefore the relationship resulting from this is different and it needs to be approached and tailored in a way that will transform that new connection from a potential through to a real client.

What you do to get things rolling is start interacting with the person you have just connected to. They might not want to buy what you offer now, but may later on. Here's a typical three step process you can follow to engage with a new LinkedIn connection.

Step one, find the type of person in your target market and send an invitation to connect.

Step two, once they accept your invitation, you thank him or her for connecting and arrange a call to work out if there is potential to help one another or do mutual business together.

Step three, now that you have started the relationship with the telephone call, aim to get to know him or her in more detail. Depending upon the location you are based in, you can plan to meet either face to face or talk via Skype.

There is no point connecting to new people just for the sake of increasing the number of your LinkedIn connections if you are not looking to engage with them and potentially do business together. But if you are serious about building a successful business strategy, here are three engagement messages you can use after you have a new connection. You ought to adapt the details according to each new case.

Option 1:

"Hi Sarah

Many thanks for connecting on LinkedIn. I always like to speak to my new connections to see how I might be able to help.

Are you around next week to schedule a call together?

Kind regards

Option 2:

"Hi Sarah

Many thanks for connecting on LinkedIn. I see we both are in real estate and may work together. Can we arrange a call next week?

Kind regards

Option 3:

"Hi Sarah

Many thanks for connecting on LinkedIn. I am looking to reach out to other local Business owners to build strategic alliances.

Would you be open to arrange a time to have a conversation to see how we might work together?

Kind regards

Make sure you always, always include the person's name in your message. Test and measure the responses and if it doesn't work, adapt and tweak the message. When you find a message that does work well because it generates positive results, keep using it. Different people will respond to different messages, some will resonate with them more than others.

But your approach shouldn't be about promoting your services as soon as you win a new connection. As with all steps generating new customers and eventually new sales, you need to find out more about the new connection both as an individual and as a business person to see if you have rapport. See how you can help him or her and explore the possibilities of working together or becoming a supplier and so on.

I was having a conversation recently with a new connection of mine. She couldn't understand why LinkedIn wasn't working and generating new sales for her. I asked her what her approach was when she wanted to acquire a new LinkedIn connection, and her reply was, *"I send a price list and information about our company's services."*

Using such an approach before you've even had a chance to speak to and get to know your new connection a little more is counterproductive. The point is, if you don't like being sold to it is important not to jump in and sell to others straight away. It won't work.

These are my Ten Rules of Engagement when approaching a new LinkedIn connection to lead them along the journey to becoming a client:

1. Never connect and pitch your services

2. Never make the approach about you, instead go for WIIFT (What's In It For Them?)

3. Always use someone's LinkedIn profile information to make a personal approach

4. Find a common thread together – resonate with them

5. Use comparisons if possible; pick out similarities; find out what is important to them

6. You are in an interruption market, build trust first

7. People buy from people, so make a human approach

8. Show you have done some research and weave this in

9. Always be positive and don't expect a response from everyone you reach out to

10. Save the selling topic until you speak to them

Let's get started by setting a strategy of aiming to speak to one new person a day. That is five new people a week, amounting to 20 new people a month and leading to 240 new people a year. Wouldn't that be a good use of your time?

If you speak to potentially 240 new people I guarantee it will generate new customers for you. Some people will buy and some won't, but if you just connect and do nothing else all I can say is that you will be wasting your time.

How to Nurture Your New and Existing LinkedIn Contacts

At this point it is worth thinking about the long term nurture of both your existing and your potential clients. Here's what I mean by this. You can export your LinkedIn connections (I'll show you how below) and add to your CRM system (Customer Relationship Management). This is a system that helps you keep in contact with your database of connections on a regular basis. It is pointless to add a new connection and have no further communication with them.

There are many such CRM systems: Salesforce; Nimble; Sugar to name a few. The one I use is Popcorn. It is UK based and it allows me to communicate regularly with all my old and new connections. I send out regular emails to my network of contacts once a month but put email campaigns together only once a quarter (it saves time, rather doing each week or month). I share out relevant information, LinkedIn updates, new features and any special offers and so on. And my approach is the same as on LinkedIn – never "sell", but try to add value with emails useful to those reading them.

Popcorn gives detailed reporting after each email so I can check out the statistics and verify the responses and actions from the reader to identify hot prospects. Connections are free to unsubscribe at any time and I genuinely get replies and new conversations leading to new customers every time I send out an email campaign. To try a month free trial of popcorn, please visit: http://www.popcornmail.co.uk/free-trial.

The difference between using LinkedIn and Popcorn as communication tools is that your LinkedIn activity goes out to a wide online audience while Popcorn provides a personalised message service going directly into the person's email box. Combining these two fantastic forms of marketing together is an exceptional way to generate new enquiries.

The new GDPR regulations came into force in May 2018. So please make sure you are compliant the new rules and have set up your CRM system accordingly and do ask your connections if they want to opt in to your communications.

There are times it is just right for people to take action and employ my services, and I get regular thanks from my network saying how useful they find my tips – a good feeling to have! Always have a call to action at the bottom of your email to make it easy for people to buy your services should they wish to do so. Also, as with putting an article together on LinkedIn – always have an engaging headline to attract the reader's interest.

Here's how you export your connections.

Along the top black bar of your LinkedIn screen click on the word **"My Network"**. On the new screen, on the left hand side of the page, click on **"Connections "**.

Manage my network

Connections   6,719

Once inside the Connections hub, go to the top right hand side corner and click the grey wording **"Manage synced and imported contacts"**. On the right hand side of the new screen, below the heading Advanced actions, click the part **"Export contacts"** wording.

Depending upon the privacy settings of your connections, you may not have all their contact details in the exported file. If so, you might need to cross reference this depending on your CRM system.

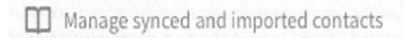

Advanced actions

 Export contacts

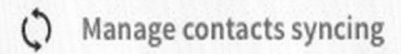 Manage contacts syncing

In the next Chapter, I will share ideas on how to reach out to a wider audience within LinkedIn and get noticed online using the Home Page. This is real time marketing as it happens so a great way to communicate, comment and share information with the online community.

7

Mapping Out a LinkedIn Strategy for Improved Publicity

Using LinkedIn is very similar to face to face networking except you don't need to travel around. The beauty of LinkedIn is that you can network from the privacy of your own office or home when it suits you. By investing time reading this book you will be able to fast track your LinkedIn marketing activity to get good and solid results and not waste time trying to find out what to do and how.

Let's jump in and take a look at LinkedIn's Home page (the page where the real time activity happens); the ideal place to be seen and build a powerful presence. You will find the Home page located on the top black bar of your LinkedIn screen next to **"My Network"**.

This is the *"social"* area of LinkedIn where real time posts, updates, jobs, profile changes, articles, group discussions and new connections are displayed. Think of it as similar to a Twitter feed where there is a non-stop stream of activity (information, posts, news, new connections) coming in from the top of the page and rolling downwards as updates are refreshed every few seconds.

You can create and post your own content or be active by clicking **"Like"**, **"Share"** or **"Comment"** on others' activity.

You can also connect to people, join LinkedIn groups and follow companies you discover from other people's updates.

Similar to the strategy when using LinkedIn groups or posts, you need to grab attention with your communication activity. If someone likes or comments on your update then it comes back up to the top of the feed which then gives you and them extra visibility.

How to Reach the Right Audience and Generate Leads via LinkedIn Home Page

It is very simple to publish updates from within LinkedIn's Home page. At the top of the Home page, click on the **"Start a post"** wording. Start typing in the box provided the content you want to send out by beginning first with an engaging headline, then add a paragraph of up to 600 characters. You can also share images, a video or a document by clicking the corresponding buttons. The image needs to be a jpeg file, the document a pdf file.

There are four crucial questions you should keep in mind before creating and sharing an update.

1. Is the content of interest to your relevant market?

2. Am I adding value to people reading the update?

3. Is it a topic relevant about your business?

4. Will it stimulate a response from the reader?

When you have dealt with the above you need to choose your hashtags. Click the blue **"Add hashtag"**, add three to five relevant keywords to categorise the content and click **"Post "**.

Add hashtag   Help the right people see your post

The Post will hit the Home Page feed and you have two options to share it further. Click the **"Share"** arrow underneath the Post. On the drop down menu click **"Share in a Post"** wording. On the new screen you have the following options.

"Anyone" – visible to anyone on LinkedIn checking the Home page

"Anyone + Twitter" – visible to anyone looking at the Home page. If you have added your Twitter account to your profile, you can tweet out at the same time

"Connections only" – visible to only your 1st line connections checking the Home page

Groups – choose any of your Groups for the Post to hit the feed inside the Group (make sure it is relevant to that particular Group). Once you have made your selection click the **"Done"** button to share.

Booster Tip: By connecting your Twitter account to your profile you can save yourself lots of time as you don't need to go into Twitter but can tweet out with a click out via LinkedIn. Here's how to add your Twitter account to your LinkedIn profile.

Along the top black bar click on the word **"Me"** and on the drop down menu click **"Settings & Privacy"**. Then on the left hand side of the screen, under the blue wording **"Account"**, click **"Partners and Services"** section and where you will see **"Twitter settings"**. Click on the grey **"Change"** button to add the details.

Third parties

Third party apps   Change

View apps you've authorized and manage data sharing   15 connected apps

Twitter settings   Change

Manage your Twitter info and activity on your LinkedIn account   Connected

You will need to have your LinkedIn password to hand at this point, and you can have up to two Twitter accounts if you have two separate businesses. Once added, click the blue **"Done"** button.

Twitter settings   Change

Manage your Twitter info and activity on your LinkedIn account   Connected

These are the Twitter accounts you've added. If you choose to share a post, the account marked "Primary" will be the one used for sharing on LinkedIn and Twitter.

@DawnAdlam   Primary   Remove

☑ Display on your profile?

Add a Twitter account

When you share your update and tweet out from LinkedIn make sure your update is less than 130 characters long so others can retweet and add their Twitter handles too.

The second option is sharing your Post as a personal message. When your Post is ready, click the **"Share"** arrow underneath the Post. On the new screen click the **"Send as a private message"** wording. Write the message which you can address to one or more than one person and click the blue

"Send".

Another cool feature on the post is to celebrate a teammate. Click on the **"Start a Post"** wording on the Home page and at the bottom click **"Celebrate a teammate"**.

On the new screen choose **"Welcome a team mate"** then follow the instructions or **"Give Kudos"** to show your appreciation to a colleague

Or you can post a job by clicking the **"Share that you' re hiring hiring"** box. From here you can choose your company page to share from and click the **"Create new job"** button and follow the instructions to share across your network.

Now let's get back to your strategy of sharing information and engaging the online community within the Home page. Aim to make it a daily habit to check out what people are talking about and join in the conversation. What you want to do is to build as much visibility as possible.

Here are five simple ideas for using LinkedIn's update section to great effect.

One: Promote other people, mention them and build visibility for them; people enjoy being praised and recommended. I always say a thank you to people attending my workshop and that I am looking forward to working with them.

Booster Tip: If you mention a 1st line connection on an update on the Home page, as you are about to start typing their name insert the @ symbol first and the name will be highlighted in blue so anyone viewing the Home page can click on their name and be directed to their profile.

Two: Share Slideshare documents – send out personalised pdf files to share and show your expertise. See Chapter 9 on how to use Slideshare to share pdf documents.

Three: Events – promote events you are either attending or organising, let people know they are welcome to attend and share the booking details.

Four: Add a Role or Position you are looking to recruit (always add an image to get my attention rather than just a line of text).

Five: Share an inspirational quote of the day to inspire people.

On all of these add up to three Hashtags to get extra visibility.

LinkedIn members can Like, Comment or Share your updates, every time they do it goes back to the top of the Home page as an update. Popular updates get hundreds sometimes tens of thousands of views, likes and comments and that therefore would help you build massive visibility and credibility.

If you want to share other people's updates on the Home page, click the blue buttons – **"Like"** or **"Comment"** or **"Share"** – underneath their Post. There are more options on updates. Click the three dots on the top right hand side of the post. In the new drop down menu you can choose to:

• Save the article to read later

• Copy the link of an update to post out

• Hide the post from your feed

• Unfollow a connection (though still connected, you will stop seeing their posts)

• Report this post

• Improve my feed

To choose the type of updates you want to receive, click on the three dots on the top of the update and select one from the drop down menu.

On the LinkedIn Pulse App you can adjust your settings to follow influencers and LinkedIn members. Pulse is similar to a daily newspaper hosting news, articles and insights from the top leaders and influencers across all industries.

You can follow the people in your industry for their personal and professional views. Apart from gaining valuable insights from other people's articles you can comment on and share them with the LinkedIn community. By doing so you raise your visibility and at the same time you add value to your LinkedIn followers and the wider community.

So there you have the Home page – make it a daily ten minute activity to get involved in the online LinkedIn community. Believe me, it is a great strategy and can definitely lead to new business opportunities.

Show Your Knowledge by Creating and Publishing Inspiring Articles Using Hashtags

Ok, so sharing other people's content is good, but how about creating and sharing your own content? This leads us nicely into publishing your own LinkedIn articles.

Booster Tip: When you create and publish your own articles, LinkedIn displays them in chronological order at the top section of your profile. They are positioned right underneath your About section and really help bring your profile to life and also propel you as the expert in your field.

I use a simple three step strategy when it comes to creating an effective content marketing plan: share relevant content; to the relevant people; and do it consistently over time to get results. It is all about aiming to create content that will help and engage your target clients. Here's how to create an article on LinkedIn.

Along the top black bar of your LinkedIn screen click **"Home"**, then underneath Start a post, click **"Write an article"**. As always, start with creating an engaging headline to get the reader's attention. Keep headlines to a short sentence of four or five words all of which will be displayed in bold lettering and deliver maximum impact.

The headline also needs to include searchable words for extra visibility as people can search articles by headlines. Next, add a relevant image relating to the topic for additional interest by clicking on the blue "+" icon. That's it; just start writing!

To create an eye catching and unique article you have a number of options within the main body of text and you will find this toolbar at the top of the screen.

Normal ∨ | **B** *I* <u>U</u> | ≣ ≣ | ❞ ✐

There are three sizes of fonts: Normal (smallest); Heading 2 (smaller); and Heading 1 (largest).

Change typefaces to emphasise a point in bold, italic or underlined text. For bold text click the **B,** for *Italics* text click the *I,* for <u>underscored</u> text click the <u>U</u>.

For lists you can either use numbers or bullet points, just click to the right of the Underscore icon.

Use the speech mark icon to separate a line of text to stand out from the main body of text.

Add hyperlinks to direct the reader from the article to your website or landing page. To hyperlink a word, highlight the word and click on the chain icon on the left and copy the URL link to your website or landing page.

Embed images, videos and photographs for visual appeal. To embed a video or image, click the grey square icon far left.

⊡ Write here. Add images or a video for visual impact.

Always have a call to action at the bottom of your article showing your readers what you want them to do next once they have read it. Ask them to call you, drop you a line or direct them to a page on your website for further information.

Booster Tip: The final part of creating an article is to add three #Hashtags. They should be relevant to and searchable keywords for the article and have replaced the old Tags. #Hashtags can be searched on mobile devices for additional visibility and Chrome is the best browser to create your articles in for reaching a larger audience.

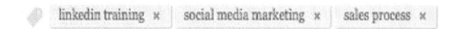

Hashtags push your LinkedIn content to a much broader audience. As with Twitter or Instagram, they *categorise* your content so it can be found and you can add hashtags in two places.

Your Posts: Go to the top black bar of the LinkedIn screen, click **"Home"**, then **"Start a post"**. Once the post is up, click the blue **"Add hashtag"** text. Add the hashtags and hit **"Post"**.

Your Articles: Go to the top black bar of the LinkedIn screen and click **"Home"**. Underneath the Start a post section, click the blue text, **"Write an article"**. Get the article ready, click the blue **"Add hashtag"** text and add the hashtags. Make sure to spell check the article one last time, just in case.

Take a deep breath, click the **"Publish"** button and off it goes live and becomes part of your profile. All your connections will get a notification to alert them. Congratulations!

You will now see all content related to this on your news feed on the Home page. Remember, you cannot remove or edit hashtags once your post or article has been published.

Booster Tip: Hashtags help your content reach a wider audience on LinkedIn. So, always add three to five hashtags when posting to create niche hashtags suitable for your brand.

LinkedIn also suggest hashtags to follow. Go to the top black bar of the LinkedIn screen and click **"Home"**. Scroll down and on the right hand side, you will see a box named Add to your feed. Click **"View all recommendations"** and then click the **"+Follow"** button to see updates in your feed.

Add to your feed   ⓘ

Do your own research on what hashtags would benefit your business and your customers. Happy hashtagging!

Booster Tip: You can, at the push of a button, share your article out to LinkedIn, Facebook and Twitter for a wider outreach. You are on your way to creating a bank of material you can go back to any time to edit, update and post out regularly to keep in touch with your followers.

Here's how to share articles. At the top right hand side of your article click the share arrow icon and on the drop down menu select to share on LinkedIn, Facebook or Twitter.

Your articles should not aim at self-promotion, but should be a testimony of your expertise and to showcase your knowledge on a particular subject. Use a mix of short and long articles. Aim to create articles every three to four weeks and send them out at different times of the day as members check LinkedIn's Home page at different times each day.

You will be notified in the Notifications hub (along the top black bar of your LinkedIn screen) when someone responds to your article which helps you engage in the conversation with him or her. You can see how many people have viewed your article, how many liked it and how many comments it has generated. Keep a track of this so you know how popular your articles are and also gauge what material and subjects are engaging with your readers.

If you have already written a series of LinkedIn articles you can save them as a draft and publish them at a later time (you can also delete an article anytime or edit and re share). The edit article button is positioned on the top right hand side of the article page.

📈 166 **views** on this post

All of your published articles are stored in chronological order on your LinkedIn profile, and you can go back to amend and update them regularly and re-publish. The latest article is on display on your profile which helps add colour and bring it to life. By clicking the **"See more articles"** text positioned underneath the article, people can view all of your previously published articles.

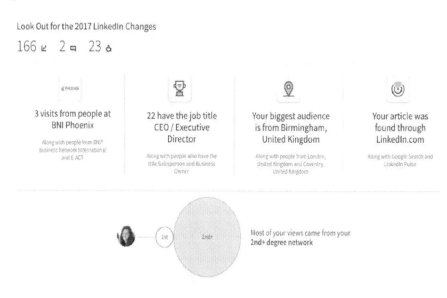

Look Out for the 2017 LinkedIn Changes

166 🗷   2 🗩   23 👍

3 visits from people at BNI Phoenix
Along with people from BNI® Business Network International and E ACT

22 have the job title CEO / Executive Director
Along with people who have the title Salesperson and Business Owner

Your biggest audience is from Birmingham, United Kingdom
Along with people from London, United Kingdom and Coventry, United Kingdom

Your article was found through LinkedIn.com
Along with Google Search and LinkedIn Pulse

Most of your views came from your 2nd+ degree network

Check the stats of your articles regularly to test and measure their success and outreach – did it engage, did members respond, share and comment? To do this, go along the top black bar of your LinkedIn screen, click on the word **"Me"** and then click **"Posts & Activity"**.

On the new screen click on the **"Articles"** wording and a list of your articles will appear. Underneath each article you will see the statistics button. Click on this to be taken to a more detailed overview of your viewers.

This is a snapshot of the job title of your article's viewers, the largest geographical area they are based in and the source the viewers used to find your article. This provides valuable feedback about your readership which you can use to target your future articles.

All your articles should relate to tips and hints on how to make the most of your area of expertise. Try to use special occasion subjects or daily events you can link with LinkedIn; and always try to go for a concise, clear call to action headline. I have, for example, generated new clients by readers who found the content of my articles relevant and, needing my help, responded to my call to action.

When one of your connections responds to your article you will get a notification so keep an eye on the Notifications hub for them. People can also like, comment or share out your article so it gets a much wider outreach and you can do the same for them.

So, flex the fingers, get ready, start writing and go publish your article!

Next, we will deal with the company page section on LinkedIn because it is crucial to your success to set up a company profile and have it running alongside your personal LinkdedIn profile.

Part III
LinkedIn For Business To Business Domination

8

Gaining Visibility and Recognition for Your Company Worldwide

Having a unique LinkedIn profile is the first crucial step to gaining visibility on LinkedIn. The second crucial step is taking advantage of your LinkedIn company page, which is your professional and corporate "website" within LinkedIn. There are four good reasons why you should have a company page on LinkedIn:

One: Increase your company's brand awareness

Two: Stay up to date regularly with news and developments in your industry

Three: Showcase your products and services

Four: Boost your career opportunities

All activity and updates pushed out from your company page will have your company's logo displayed, not your photograph. This will help you build additional brand visibility as well. Your company's activity is displayed in chronological order which makes it easy for LinkedIn members to see your previous updates any time.

Here's what you need in order to set up your company page on LinkedIn:

• You must have a personal LinkedIn profile set up with your real full name and that is over seven days old

• You need to have a minimum of ten LinkedIn connections on your profile

• You own or are a current employee of a business which you state in the Experience section on your LinkedIn profile

• You have included your business email address in your LinkedIn account settings

• Your company domain (your email address) can only be used for setting up and associated with one company page

Don't miss out on having an additional corporate presence within LinkedIn and getting that extra brand visibility.

How to Set Up a Fitting LinkedIn Page for Your Company

Along the top black bar of your LinkedIn screen click on the **"Work"** icon. On the drop down menu, right at the very bottom of it, click the wording **"Create a Company Page"**. Follow the instructions by adding all the relevant details as laid out below.

Company Name – this is self-explanatory.

LinkedIn public URL – this is unique to your company and once set it cannot be changed. LinkedIn users and, what's more, all search engines will use this unique URL to find your page. Use it wisely.

Tick the verify box and click the blue **"Create page"** button. Follow the instructions adding all the relevant details below.

Your email address – this is self-explanatory, verify you are the official representative and click the blue **"Continue"** button. Carry on working through all the required elements as below.

Description – tell your brand story using between a minimum of 250 and a maximum of 2000 words. Google preview up to 156 characters so make sure you have included relevant searchable words in your description.

Designated administrators – these are other members of your company who can edit the company page and send out updates. You must be connected to members in order to appoint them as administrators. Depending upon the size of your company you can share the responsibilities of sending out regular posts and updates with a team of people. But make sure you have a clear strategy on how this would work so you maximise the result, minimise the time spent and there is no duplication from the team. Regular updates daily or every other day work best for boosting your brand visibility.

Add an Image – bring your LinkedIn company page to life and create a recognizable banner across the top part of your company page section. Remember, the image needs to be relevant to your industry to give that professional and compelling first impression. For best quality, the image needs to be 646 x 220 PNG, JPEG or GIF maximum size of 2MB.

Add your Logo – depending on the shape of your company's logo, choose square or landscape to best present your brand. If your logo is in a wide format choose the landscape option to display it; if it is in tall format choose the square option. You don't want to use a tiny logo that isn't visible.

Specialities – use SEO searchable keywords or phrases relating to your products and services. These are individual words that you can be searched for, similar to the keywords used in your LinkedIn personal profile.

Featured Groups – if you are a member or manager of a group, add the group's details on the company page so members of other groups and your followers looking at your company page have the option to join that group too.

When you have completed all the details click the blue **"Publish"** button.

The Secret of Using LinkedIn Showcase Pages to Increase Output and Cross Sell More of Your Products and Services

Showcase pages are a fantastic additional feature to your LinkedIn company page. There are three advantages to creating Showcase pages.

First, by creating a dedicated page for each aspect of your business and with its own message you can share relevant content with a particular audience. Second, you give LinkedIn members a chance to follow those aspects of your business they value most. Third, the ability to highlight your individual brand and deliver updates directly in the feed of your followers across mobile, tablet and desktop devices.

You can create up to ten Showcase pages and attract a distinct set of followers to each separate page and push out relevant information to that particular set of followers. Because each Showcase page can have a different image relevant to a particular service, you can cross sell your other services and sub brands and, ultimately, reach out to a wider audience. Here's how to create a Showcase page.

Along the top black bar of your LinkedIn screen, click on the word **"Me"**. On the drop down menu, underneath the word MANAGE, choose the company page you want to add the Showcase Page to. Once on the company page, go to the top right hand side of the page and click the grey **"Admin tools"** wording and on the drop down menu click **"Create Showcase Page"**. A pop up window will appear; add the relevant details for the showcase page you want, click **"Create page"** and you are good to go.

Booster Tip: Showcase company pages are useful if you offer multiple services. For example, as a web design company you might offer web design, SEO and so on. Create a series of Showcase pages where you can share further content, start building relationships and separate out your services to cross sell from the company page.

Once you have created your company page on LinkedIn you need to attract and gain followers because they will be your brand ambassadors. The tip below can help a great deal.

Booster Tip: For further outreach you can add a company button, which is a hyperlink linked directly to your LinkedIn company page. Think about adding this to your email footer, blog or website alongside the message, *"Click here to follow our c ompany page on LinkedIn for regular Industry updates"*. Here's how.

First, cut and paste this link into your web browser to get the code details to create your LinkedIn company button: https://developer.linkedin.com/plugins/follow-company. You will need your LinkedIn password to set this up. Once this is setup, you can take your company branding one step further by adding your logo to your LinkedIn profile.

Second, go along the top black bar of your LinkedIn screen; click on the word **"Me"**. Click **"View profile"** and scroll down to the relevant Experience section of your profile. Click on the blue edit pencil on the right hand side of your screen. Retype the company name in the Company box.

Title

Bizlinks Coach / Social Media Training / LinkedIn Training / Lead Generation

Company

 TheBizlinks

LinkedIn will give you a list of possible companies similar to yours, click on the relevant company and the logo will automatically be added. Each time someone clicks on the logo they will be directed to your company page, where they can find out more about and also follow your company.

You are now set up and good to go with your marketing activity. Share out regular updates daily or every two days and, remember, by sending out little updates often you get more and more engagement and followers. For example, you can add value with a mix of short snappy updates such as:

• Promotional material and special offers

• Top tip documents showcasing your expertise

• Testimonials and inspiring posts

• Promoting members in your network

• Respond to trends or hot topics to engage with the online community

• Relevant videos (YouTube videos get a 75% share rate)

How to Share Updates from Your LinkedIn Company Page and Add Value to Your Business Network

Posting content on LinkedIn is easy and, what's more, statistics show you will get twice the engagement with your audience when you attach a relevant image or link. Here's how to do it.

Along the top black bar of your LinkedIn screen, click on the word **"Me"**. On the drop down menu choose the company page you want to share an update from. Once on the company page, click the **"Start a post"** box and enter an attention grabbing headline. You can also attach a photograph by clicking the camera icon, add a video link by clicking the video icon or attach a document by clicking the document icon.

Make sure your article or update is relevant and appeals to your connections or potential audience you are targeting. Click the blue **"Post"** button and choose the Post settings on the drop down menu either Public or Targeted Audience.

The targeted audience is based on different demographics, for example: Language; Company Size; Geography and so on. Make sure your update is directly relevant and appeals to these demographics. You need at least 300 company followers to enable the targeted share. Make sure to click the **"Allow comments on this post button"** so you can check engagement and respond to comments. Click **"Done"** to share. Companies that post content weekly double engagement with users.

You can also search and follow companies you are interested in to keep up to date with their activities and engage with them by liking, sharing or commenting on their updates.

To search for other companies, go along the top black bar of your LinkedIn screen and click the **"Search"** box. On the new screen click **"More"** and on the drop down list click **"Companies"**.

Click the "Companies" button and on the new screen type the name of the company you want to follow. As you start typing, a list of companies will appear; click on the relevant one to be taken to that company's LinkedIn page. Once on the company page click the blue "Follow" button to start seeing their content in your newsfeed.

Booster Tip: You know your company domain (email address) can only be used once to set up a company page and that you can only have one page relating to your business. An alternative to this is setting up a new LinkedIn group relating to your company services. This means you can now communicate with a targeted group of people within a group rather than the followers on a Company page. Your group will be visible to all LinkedIn members and positioned at the bottom of your profile.

How to Measure and Fine Tune the Performance of Your LinkedIn Company Page

With all the effort you have put in after setting up a company page and posting information out regularly, it is crucial to see how well your LinkedIn company page is performing. It's easy to check and analyse this information. Here's how.

Along the top black bar of your LinkedIn screen, click on the word **"Me"**. On the drop down menu click the company page want to check. Click the **"Analytics"** button on top left hand side of the company page screen and a dropdown menu will appear; you now have access to detailed information on your company's engagement and activity including:

• Visitors – last 30 days highlights from page views and custom button clicks to visitor demographics, job function and unique visitors

• Updates – last 30 days update highlights from percentage of reactions to comments and shares

• Followers – last 30 days follower highlights of your total followers and of new followers

By clicking on the black arrow next to the date you can reset the time range of all these analytics. It would give you a detailed history from the last seven days through to the last 12 months. You can see what content is generating interest.

The higher the numbers on each of these sections the more visibility you will achieve and increase the chance of people wanting to buy from you. Next to the Analytics button you will see the Activity button.

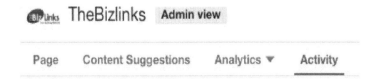

This will show you an update of all the social notifications. From here you can drill down deeper and check out at a glance the responses to your activity. This includes the Reactions, Shares, and Mentions your updates have generated. If people are gaining value from the information you create then they will like, comment and share which then gets pushed out to their network delivering greater visibility for you. More activity means more visibility, more followers and, ultimately, more marketing opportunities to a much wider network.

It's similar to throwing a pebble in a pond – the ripples reach out further and further. If your updates are not grabbing attention or are perceived of adding no real value, it is then best to change the content you send out to make sure it is engaging and also likely to be shared by your readers.

LinkedIn also suggests content for you to share. On your company page click the **"Content Suggestions"** wording.

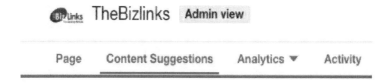

On the new screen you can choose an industry and add any topic you are interested by clicking the **"Add a topic"** wording. You'll see a list of trending topics over the last 15 days which you can share using the **"Share"** button. This will get you additional visibility for your company apart from being another way of engaging with your followers.

Hold on though, there is more you can do with your company page on LinkedIn.

How to Market Your Company on LinkedIn for Greater Business Growth and Profit

You can use paid advertising within the LinkedIn platform and have your content going out into the feed across every device and not only from your company page. This is a premium paid service, where you can target a unique audience, create and post ads and set your own budget and control your spend. In this way you can direct your messages to the right audience.

First, take a look at the options available. Go along the top black bar of your LinkedIn screen, and on the far right hand side click on the **"Work"** icon. On the dropdown menu and on the pop up window that appears, click **"Advertise"** and you can check the options, benefits and the costs involved.

Visit more LinkedIn products

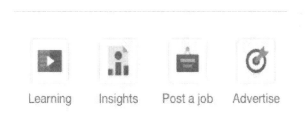

Learning   Insights   Post a job   Advertise

The most important question you need to sort out before getting started is to specify who you want to target. Of over 500 million LinkedIn users you can target a unique audience by selecting:

• Job function

• Job title

• Seniority

• Skills

• Company name

• Company industry

• Company size

You can also reach members across a wide range of education programmes and institutions including school, degree and field of study.

Sponsored Content: This is the part where you can promote your company updates to targeted audiences on your desktop, mobile and tablet to drive awareness and generate new leads on the news feed. The benefits are:

• Send company's updates to more people to attract new followers

• Reach the right audience using comprehensive targeting options

• Get your message out on every device

• Set your own budget be it cost per click or per impression options

• Use Direct Sponsored Content to easily test your messaging

• Track the number of leads from your ads on LinkedIn with conversion tracking

Follow the link for more details: https://business.linkedin.com/marketing-solutions/native-advertising.

Sponsored InMail: Here you send personalised messages to prospects where you can target audiences with relevant content delivered through LinkedIn messenger. Responsive design on these emails means your call to action is always visible and sponsored InMail messages are only delivered when members are active on LinkedIn to ensure you message gets noticed. The benefits are:

• Boost registrations with personalised invites to online or offline events

• Drive conversation with targeted product and service promotions

• Promote content downloading infographics, white papers, eBooks and more

Follow the link for more details: https://business.linkedin.com/marketing-solutions/sponsored-inmail.

LinkedIn Text Ads: Here you can create Text Adverts to get in front of the right audience to drive them to your website or landing pages. These ads are easy to create, you can set your own budget with no long term commitments and they are based on PPC – pay per click. These are visible on the home page and the benefits are:

• Target the specific audience you want to reach

• Set your own budget without committing to long-term ad campaigns

• Pay for only the ads that work be it pay per click or per impression

• Track the number of leads you get from your ads on LinkedIn with conversation tracking

Follow the link for more details: https://business.linkedin.com/marketing-solutions/ppc-advertising.

Dynamic Ads: Here you can create ads that drive responses unique to your audience's activity. You can target decision makers and personalise your message with calls to action. These are visible on the home page. The benefits are:

• Select and target the audiences you want to reach based on a wide range of professional targeting criteria including company, skills, interests, and more

• Measure your performance by analysing campaign-reporting metrics provided by your LinkedIn account and fine-tune your ads

• Grow your company reach by building relationships and grow your company's LinkedIn follower count using unique ad formats and "Follow Company" CTAs

Follow the link for more details: https://business.linkedin.com/marketing-solutions/dynamic-ads

There is also an option to target your specific list of priority accounts with a new ABM tool which matches up to 30,000 target accounts to LinkedIn company pages where you can run ad campaigns to influencers and decision makers. This option is only available to LinkedIn – assisted clients (it is a paid support service).

Follow the link for more details: https://business.linkedin.com/marketing-solutions/ad-targeting/account-targeting

Ok, you can now plan your paid online marketing activity should you wish. Remember, your marketing activity always needs to be tested and measured regularly. Being active with and conducting marketing campaigns isn't enough; you need to see tangible results and I will show you more simple yet effective ways to measure responses from your LinkedIn activity.

Next up we will be looking at innovative ways to make the most of your LinkedIn activity whilst minimising the time investment, making sure you get the results you are looking for and building up that pipeline of new opportunities.

9

How to Get the Most Out of Your LinkedIn Activity without Costing You Masses of Time and Headache

Marketing and advertising is the business of promoting and selling your products or services and a large part of it is linked to market research. It is a case of testing and measuring your activity to help create demand for and bring in sales. Sitting and waiting for the phone to ring or customers to knock on your door never works.

LinkedIn is the perfect online opportunity to showcase your expertise with well-crafted documents that will add value to and help other people. In return, this would get you noticed and drive people to your LinkedIn profile or to your website where they can see what you do and how you can help them. There is a misconception that if people are busy creating marketing material then it must work for them.

But how do you know if your marketing material is working? Do you analyse the responses you are getting? No one wants to spend huge amounts of time and money with zero sales or, at least, interest being generated. This is where creating a LinkedIn marketing strategy alongside your offline marketing activities can work brilliantly in increasing your income stream.

LinkedIn is a valuable tool which enables you to check out all your marketing activity statistics within the LinkedIn platform including Updates, Posts, Profile Views, Slideshare and your interaction via LinkedIn's Home page. In this way, you can see what material is meaningful to your network and if it is making an impact. And if it isn't, you need to rethink and adapt your content strategy to benefit you and your network.

There are a number of tracking options to give an overview of the outreach and pulling power of your LinkedIn efforts.

One: Who has viewed your profile. Along the top black bar of your LinkedIn screen click on the word **"Me"**. On the drop down menu click **"View profile"**. Underneath the About section, you'll find Your Dashboard which only you can see.

Click on the **"Who viewed your profile"** grey wording to see the list of people who have checked your profile. The free version of LinkedIn allows you to see only the last five people; on the Premium version you can see all who have visited your profile in the last 90 days. Checking the number of visits on your profile helps you track if your activity has raised awareness and generated traffic to your LinkedIn page.

When you click the **"Search appearances"** box you can see the weekly number of times your profile appeared in search results. Underneath this you can then see where people who searched you work, their profession and the keyword they used leading to you.

If you have a small network of connections, concentrate on building and expanding the network first, so more people can see your activity and be attracted to your profile. If you are not seeing an increase in your profile views your marketing activity isn't hitting the mark and you, therefore, need to rethink your LinkedIn strategy.

One good practice proven to bring results is sending the viewers of your profile a message thanking them for visiting your profile and offering to connect with or help them. On the four LinkedIn premium versions available you have far more information on the viewers.

Here's the question you need to tackle: is it crucial to your business to know who has viewed your profile? If yes, you should consider upgrading. My take on this is: if people are looking at my profile, it is great; if they want to connect, fantastic; if they don't then that's fine, too. I don't track who is looking at me in more detail as I figure if they want to connect to me then they will make an approach.

Two: Number of views of your post. On the same dashboard as above the second box shows you how many people have viewed your post. Click the **"Posts"** box to see a list of your most recent posts. The number of views on your last update is a crucial indicator because more views means more opportunities for people to buy from you.

Three: Notifications section. Your will find this along the top black bar of your LinkedIn screen next to Messaging. Click **"Notifications"** and you can see responses on what you have commented on or shared, all of which will be flagged up here.

You will also be able to see when anyone mentions your name. Keeping an eye daily on this means you won't miss any opportunities to engage with and respond to the online community. From here you can also see all your activity in the most recent order.

Any changes happening to your network connections will also show on the Notifications page so you can be informed of job and profile updates of your connections. You can see who is celebrating their birthday and can wish them many happy returns. This means you have a real time and up to date database where you can interact directly and stay in touch with your contacts.

Four: The statistics of your articles will help you see how many people have read your LinkedIn articles and what the feedback was. Here's how to get there.

Along the top black bar of your LinkedIn screen, click on the word **"Me"**. On the drop-down menu click **"View profile"** and underneath your dashboard, at Your Articles & Activity section, click on the blue wording **"See all articles"**. You will be taken to all your articles and where you can see the numbers of views, clicks, for each article.

If there were no viewers or no responses from your article you will need to make changes as it didn't connect with the online community. Change the photograph or the headline and copy and re-share to re-engage your audience. As articles are part of your marketing strategy you want to share information of interest along with calls to action which leads to people engaging and responding with you. If you are posting to self-promote only, it will turn off your connections and they will not respond.

You are the expert in your field; show and share your knowledge and expertise with your followers publishing articles on LinkedIn. Try to add value with tips and insights aiming to create a response. One response would be to write a thank you message to someone who liked or commented on your LinkedIn article – it is a great response to get and like a snowball effect people would want to read what else you have to say next time around.

More importantly, being able to see who has liked, commented on or shared your articles helps you start a dialogue together. I would recommend publishing an article on LinkedIn once every three or four weeks. Regular sharing of information increases tremendously your visibility on LinkedIn and positions you as someone who is seriously interested in others and wants to help them succeed.

Always keep adapting and changing the information you send out to keep it relevant and fresh. Think of all the elements to your business and pick a relevant topic to discuss, or give tips and *how to* topics. Marketing is about consistency by sending out useful material regularly, and when you do so you'll start getting comments and responses guaranteed.

Five: An overview of your company page. Along the top black bar of your LinkedIn screen, click on the word **"Me"**. On the drop down menu, under the MANAGE wording, click on the company page you want to check. Once on the company page click the **"Analytics"** wording for all the details.

As a snapshot you can check updates on Visitors, Updates and Followers.

Visitors: You can see the data for the last 30 days – Page views, Unique visitors, Custom button clicks.

Updates: You can see the data for the last 30 days – Reactions, Comments and Shares.

Followers: You can see the data for the last 30 days – Total followers and the follower demographics by location.

As an addition you can also see Companies to Track – See how your followers and updates compare to companies similar to your company.

By tracking these metrics you can see if the LinkedIn activity from your company page is working, and, as a result, if your visibility is up or down. You want to get noticed and drive more traffic and viewers to your profile or website so potential clients can see what you do and how you can help them and their business.

Six: Slideshare views. Once you have uploaded your documents to Slideshare you have detailed analytics on your viewers including volume of viewers and their geographical location. Along the top black bar of your LinkedIn screen, on the far right hand side, click on the **"Work"** icon. On the drop menu click **"Slideshare"**.

Within Slideshare hover over your image, which is on the top right hand corner of your screen, and on the dropdown menu click on the orange **"My uploads"** button. Select the document you want to see the results of and at the bottom of the document, hover over the icons and click **"View Detailed Analytics"**.

From here you can see the source of your viewers, their number, the country they came from and any actions they took regarding your documents. You can use all this data as a highly effective market research tool to gauge how your followers are interacting with your marketing materials and promoting activity.

If it appeals to your follower's needs they will respond to your call to action – be it by calling you, emailing you, requesting a brochure and so on. Marketing isn't about force selling to people; it is about getting their attention first by giving them nuggets of value to pique their interest. LinkedIn is a different form of marketing because it is all online which means you can share your information to a much wider online audience.

For example, instead of mailing out a brochure to your prospects, you produce a pdf version of it and then share it online as an update, a post or upload it as a Slideshare document; or all three. You get the message out there to a larger audience at the click of a button.

All your activity within LinkedIn drives members to your profile which gives them an opportunity to buy from you. You may have created a fantastic LinkedIn profile, but if no one ever finds it you are limiting your chances of people buying from you.

Overall, you can see the engagement your activity has generated, such as who liked your update, who left a comment and what they said. It is a good way to keep an eye on what type of activity is generating interest from your network of followers. Out of courtesy, always respond to and answer any questions or start a conversation with the person who is commenting. All this goes back to the principle of starting and building relationships which is one of the first crucial steps in the sales process. Here's how.

Along the top black bar of your LinkedIn screen, click on the word **"Me"**. On the drop-down menu click **"View profile"** and scroll down to Your Articles & Activity section. Click **"See all activity"** wording located underneath. On the new screen click the **"All activity"** wording and you can see in chronological order, the most recent first, all your updates and the number of likes and comments people have made.

Dawn's Activity

All activity   Articles   Posts   Documents

Other people can view your recent activity from your LinkedIn profile and you can do the same from theirs. If you want to view someone's recent activity, you can search for a person by name along the top black bar of your LinkedIn screen using the white search box. Once you are on that person's profile, click the **"See all activity"** wording, as described above, and you can see what they have been talking about and sharing on LinkedIn. You can anytime respond and comment on their activity.

I have generated new clients by sharing their content, messaging them about it and then speaking to them. One of my best referrals came from someone who had been in one of my workshops many months ago. She saw a comment I had posted on LinkedIn's Home page and contacted me for some advice on an unrelated topic. She passed my details to one of her friends who runs the marketing department for a £25 million turnover company. We had a conversation together and they became my client. The moral of the story is: Go out there and get noticed!

In the next chapter you will learn the pros and cons of LinkedIn groups and how to use them to your advantage, because it is where your target market and potential clients will be hanging out. Whether local or specific industry type, groups are easy to find and join and, what's more, you may even want to start your own LinkedIn group.

10

Harnessing the Tremendous Power of LinkedIn Groups to Help Your Business Grow and Be Unstoppable

---

Groups are smaller communities within LinkedIn consisting of like-minded professionals who are part of the same industry or share similar interests as you. Communicating with tens of thousands of people is a challenge; communicating with people smaller pockets of communities increases dramatically the chances of you building visibility faster and with good results.

There are four main reasons why you should consider joining a LinkedIn group. You can:

• Post discussions to gain visibility

• View jobs and find a new position

• Network, connect and interact with group members

• Above all, share your expertise and establish yourself as an industry expert and trend setter in your field

How to Find Groups that Are an Ideal Fit for Your Business Growth

The trouble with LinkedIn groups is there are hundreds of thousands of them; at the last count there were nearly two million active ones! You want to find and join particular groups that would benefit you and your business. In order to locate groups that are right for you and your business, you should base your search on three criteria.

First: Your target market groups. Choose national and regional LinkedIn groups which contain your prospective clients. For example, if you are a commercial builder based in the US then join a US based commercial property group. There are many types of commercial property groups, so do some research to find the best one for you.

Second: Regional local business groups. These are ideal for reaching out and connecting with other local businesses in your area. If you network in local groups it is easier and faster to connect, arrange meetings and do business locally.

Third: Peer groups. These groups are useful to share ideas, keep up to date with and stay on top of the latest trends and news within your industry. If you network and interact with industry leaders it keeps you ahead of the competition.

When conducting a search for a LinkedIn, group don't forget to include the country you want to base your search in. If you use the default worldwide search you will waste valuable time searching for groups that are not relevant to you. You can also discover new groups from the ones LinkedIn would suggest.

There are three ways to search for groups to join.

One: Along the top black bar of your LinkedIn screen, click in the search box on the top left hand side of the black bar. A choice of filters will appear, click **"Groups"**.

(People) (Jobs) (Content) (Companies) (Schools) (Groups)

On the new screen a list of all the groups will appear. Type the country and group description into the white search bar and start discovering new groups to join and network in LinkedIn.

Two: Along the top black bar of your LinkedIn screen, click the word **"Work"** and on the drop down menu click **"Groups"**. At the bottom of the screen click the blue **"Search"** wording and repeat as above to search for a new group.

Search other trusted communities that share and support your goals.

Three: Check the groups your LinkedIn connections are in. Here's how. Go to the profile of one of your 1st line connections and then scroll right to the bottom. Click the blue **"See all"** wording. On the new screen click the word **"Groups"** to see a list of the groups they are in. Join any suiting you.

Do your homework before joining a group. Check its activity to find out if it is an active group with plenty of discussions and members. Having more members in a group means wider visibility and reach for you. When checking a group, on the right hand side of the group page you will be able to see information such as the rules about and how many members there are in the group. Each group has different rules so check these out before asking to join.

Once you request to join, your request will go to the administrators for approval. LinkedIn have updated the group privacy settings and there are no open LinkedIn groups anymore. All public groups have now moved across to private groups and all applications to join have to be approved first.

Once you have been accepted into the group there should be no hard "selling" or self-promotion tactics. The group manager can remove you from the group if you do not follow the group's rules.

All groups have exactly the same layout and are easy to navigate once you have joined. Once you are inside the group you can get access to the two vital functions: Conversations and Jobs. I'll show next how you can use these vital functions to your benefit.

Becoming a Top Contributor for Record High Profile Views

Joining a LinkedIn group and being an active member in it gives you the opportunity to raise your profile and be seen as the expert in your field, making you the "go to" person for advice. Group conversations are about engaging with other members and not for self-promotion though.

As a new member of a LinkedIn group, it is better to contribute first to other people's conversations rather than diving in straight away with your own discussions. To start with, look at what daily conversations are taking place and get a feel about the group.

Once you have gained confidence in contributing to conversations start posting your own. Make them helpful and relevant to the topic discussed aiming to add real benefit to the group members. Here are some useful ideas for starting engaging conversations:

• Ask open questions

• Poll the group for opinions and feedback

• Share interesting, relevant information

• Ask for help if you need a recommended supplier

• Ask for help if you need market research

Posting for the sake of it, apart from generating no interest, may be classed as spam and can lead to the owner of the group blocking you from posting in the future. Always ask before posting this question: *"Am I adding value that would benefit both the members within the group and those of the wider network?"* If the answer is no, don't post the content yet, go back and edit it. Here's how to get started.

Along the top black bar on your LinkedIn screen, click on the word **"Work"** and on the drop down menu click **"Groups"**. On the new screen, your list of groups will appear. Click on the group you want to engage with. Once inside the group click **"Start a new conversation in this group"**.

As with the Home page, always aim to get attention with a good conversation title and remember to add three hashtags for boosting visibility. Add an image, video or document by clicking on one of the icons on the right hand side.

Apart from written details, you can bring your conversations to life by adding links to useful articles, videos and good images. To add an image in your conversation, click on the camera icon on the bottom left hand side of the text box. To add a video link, click on the video icon. Once you have spell checked your conversation, click on the blue **"Post"** button on the bottom right hand side of the text box and voila! – out it gets posted to the whole group.

If you want to join another member's conversation in the group, underneath their conversation box click **"Like"** (they will get a notification you have liked their conversation) or you can comment directly. To do this, click **"Comment"** and type your reply in the white conversation box. The member will get a notification you have commented and your reply will be visible to all the group members.

You can also save, copy the link of or report the post by clicking the three dots on the top right of the post and selecting from the drop down menu. The more active you are in a group the more visible you will become. By commenting regularly on other people's conversations and by starting your own conversations, you can get to increase the number of your LinkedIn profile views by up to 400%!

Secret Tips to Make Valuable Connections Through LinkedIn Groups

Within the group you will be able to see all its members which is extremely useful to prospect for new connections. In order to check out the group members, click the word **"Work"** along the top black bar of your LinkedIn screen, then on the drop down menu click **"Groups"**. Choose a group and once inside the group page, on the right hand side of your screen you will see the number of members – in this example it shows as **"8,559 members"**. Click on the **"See all"** wording.

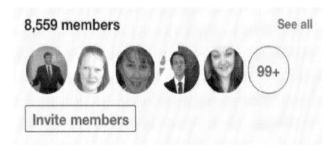

This will take you to the list of all the group members which, unfortunately, is not in alphabetical order. But you now have access to send a message to anyone in the LinkedIn group and you don't have to be directly connected to them. This is where one's LinkedIn profile headline is so handy because you will be able to see it alongside the name and the photograph of each group member.

Identify people from the list of members you would like to add to your network and you can send them a personalised message. You do this by clicking the **"Message"** button on the right hand side of their photo.

Keep repeating the process working your way through the group members to bring them into your network. You can send up to 15 messages per month within each group. A simple connection request message example to use can be:

"Dear Mo

W e are both in the Brummies group on LinkedIn and are also based in the same area. May I have your permission to connect, please?

Kind regards

Three things will happen once you send a request: one, they will ignore you; two, they will connect; or, three, they will respond and ask you to connect to them. If any of the last two happens don't leave it at that, start the next step in the communication process.

It is getting to know a new LinkedIn connection better that will bring new business opportunities your way. The most important thing, once you have a new connection, would be to always, always follow up with them. Adding them to your LinkedIn network and doing nothing else will not generate the start of a relationship. Acquiring a new connection is the first touch point, arranging a conversation or setting up a meeting will be the next touch point in moving them up the ladder towards becoming a client.

Think about your prospecting activity and decide how much time you can allocate every week to schedule telephone conversations. You can then relate that to how many people you ask to connect. Don't try to connect to 20 people at a time if you cannot find the time to arrange calling and speak to each of them.

A steady and regular stream of new connections works best because you can pencil in time to organise conversations. Work your way through one group at a time and measure how many connection requests you send, how many respond and how many conversations you have had.

For example, sending two new connection requests a day on LinkedIn would result in ten a week, which amounts to 40 a month which means up to 40 new people to connect to; and all it takes to do this is five minutes of your time each day. Sending regular requests has a huge impact when compared to dipping in and out without a clear strategy of building your network; it is how you keep a flow of new people to speak to.

There are two easy methods of using LinkedIn groups to prospect. One, from one's LinkedIn profile you can see what group or groups he or she is a member of. You join that group, find him or her in the member section then send a direct message. Two, search through the members of a particular LinkedIn group for those who would be good connections for you, and once you locate them you message them directly.

The logo of every LinkedIn group you are a member of will be displayed at the bottom of your LinkedIn profile. LinkedIn members can see which groups you are in and how active you are in the LinkedIn community. If you don't belong to any LinkedIn groups the perception could be that you are not interested in engaging with local activities or other LinkedIn members.

If you want to see what groups your 1st line connections are in, go to their LinkedIn profile. Once there, scroll right to the bottom and click the blue **"See all"** wording, which is situated under the screen named Following. Click the **"Groups"** button and a list of the groups each of your connections is in will appear.

Following

Companies   **Groups**   Schools

You can also change the frequency of daily or weekly digests you receive from each group. To do this, go first to the particular group you want digests from, and once inside the group, click on the three dots on the right hand side of the group name.

On the drop down menu click **"Update your settings"** and on the new screen decide whether the group members can message you, if you want the group to appear on your profile and the type of communication and activity you want to see. Most group members will not be your 1st line connections, but by allowing all group members to message you, you pave the way for new connection requests and new conversations. You can control the flow of emails by tweaking the email frequency from the group so you don't get deluged with content you don't want.

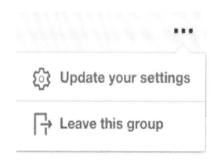

A sensible number of LinkedIn groups to belong to would be between three and six. It's how you can keep up to date with information, have an impact and create visibility locally or wider afield yet without being deluged with too much content and information.

As an active user of LinkedIn I would expect to see at least two or three groups on your LinkedIn profile you are active or have an interest in, this would show me you play a part in the online community of LinkedIn.

You can leave a group, at any point you want, by clicking on the three dots as explained above.

How to Start Your Own Group and Become a True Trailblazer in Your Industry

Have you ever thought of starting your own group? This is not a bad idea at all. Here are three main reasons you should consider it.

First, as the owner of a LinkedIn group you have the power to invite, accept or reject applications from people to join. In this way, you raise your visibility and, more importantly, you surround yourself with serious business professionals.

Second, by setting up a specific LinkedIn group relevant to a particular industry you can position yourself as the expert in your field, invite other like-minded professionals to join and create a power hub.

Third, by creating an internal company group to communicate within your own business you can bring all the employees together in one place something which can work well if you have multi sites.

Managing a LinkedIn group can be time consuming as you need to send regular invites to join to keep the group growing and evolving, along with accepting requests to join. Regular communication alongside posting relevant content and discussions are essential. How much time you can devote to the administration of the group each week will depend on how popular and well promoted your group is.

You need to be an active member of the group showing ownership of and being visible in it on a regular basis. How would this fit in with your marketing activity and what you want to achieve? Will becoming a LinkedIn group influencer raise your profile and generate interest? Yes, it will. Here's how to set up your own LinkedIn group.

Along the top black bar of your LinkedIn screen, click the word **"Work"** and on the drop down menu click **"Groups"**. On the top right hand side of the screen, click the blue wording **"Create a new group"**.

Create a new group

You will be taken to a new window, fill the requested information (a red asterisk means the information is required). Create a name for your group, add a logo and set out the rules and introduction for members joining. It's as simple as that!

You can make your group Listed or Unlisted. Unlisted groups are visible to everyone on LinkedIn; Listed, to group members only. If the group is listed it can be found in searches and will also be visible on members' profiles. If unlisted, it will not be the case.

To change the listing, click the edit pencil next to **"About this Group"**. On the new screen select the group type clicking **"Listed"** or **"Unlisted"** and click **"Save"**.

The same rules about avoiding self-promotion apply in each group; the crucial thing is to think of ways of adding value with conversations. As a group manager you can decide what content is allowed and you can remove any discussions if you think they are not suitable.

Create a strategy for regular postings and communications within the group to keep members interested and engaged. As a LinkedIn group manager, your details are visible to all the group members so your profile is raised considerably. Will members flock to join your group? With tens of millions of potential users it may take some effort and planning to make it happen, but it will happen.

In the next section I will show you how to generate more members and create new connections and opportunities.

How to Build a Powerful Hub of Likeminded Professionals Promoting Your LinkedIn Group

What needs to happen after you set up your own LinkedIn group is that it needs to build traction. Let's look at the options online digital marketing provides as the quickest and easiest method of promoting your group and, best of all, it being free. Here's how to do it.

Along the top black bar of your LinkedIn screen, click the word **"Work"** and on the drop down menu click **"Groups"**. Choose the group you want to invite connections to join and on the right hand side of your screen click the box **"Invite members"**.

8,559 members   See all

99+

Invite members

From here a list of your connections will appear, tick the box of the people you would like to invite and then click the blue **"Invite"** button (this applies to any groups you belong to). You can send multiple invites in one go. You can also search through your connections to select who to invite. All requestes to join a group will still require admin approval.

You want to keep adding new members along the way to keep the group vibrant and not static unless it is an internal group with members from your own company, in which case this doesn't apply.

Repeat the inviting activity once a week; it takes very little time to do it. See it as a longer term time investment so you can have a wider outreach to engage online and invite people to join your group. As group manager, you also get to filter and approve every applicant who requests to join which gives you more opportunities to speak and engage with new people. You also have the power to control the conversations and can delete any inappropriate comments should that happen.

Groups definitely have a part to play in becoming part of your regular LinkedIn activity, because it is all about finding and connecting to new people, raising your visibility and getting noticed a lot more.

Ultimately, you should think about setting up your own group. But remember, managing a group is time demanding, so think this through before setting one up; spend time in other groups first to see how they operate.

Such is the success of one of my local LinkedIn groups, the membership of the group has grown to over 8000 members and they have plenty of conversations and offer lots of support. Due to popular demand they have moved offline and now meet face to face once a month. This tactic is really powerful as the members can meet regularly to network and build good business relationships together leading to new business opportunities. This is the cornerstone to generating new business: connect, talk to and try to meet face to face with new people.

I hope this chapter has given you an overview of the value of narrowing down the millions of LinkedIn users in your country to a more targeted and focused method of finding and connecting to groups of people rather than using the needle in a haystack approach!

You can use LinkedIn groups to search for and message members and make new connections who will definitely be of great benefit in reaching out to. Get recognised as the expert in your field with well thought out conversations to help and add value to as many people as possible – it is the key to using the immense potential of LinkedIn groups effectively.

In the next chapter I will be sharing with you ways to search and apply for jobs using LinkedIn. If you are not looking to find your next role or challenge, skip this chapter and move on to more tips on using this fantastic online platform.

Well done so far. You are well over three quarters of the way through and you are making great headway, a pat on the back, take a deep breath and let's carry on!

Part IV
LinkedIn Makeover For Job And Recruitment Success

11

How to Crack the Job Market and Land Your Dream Job Using LinkedIn

If you want to use LinkedIn to find a job you need create a different strategy and approach. Because it's all about making it easy for a potential employer to see both the skills you have and the value you would bring to the company.

The first place to get started is your LinkedIn profile and once you have updated and polished it; your activity alongside being proactive will make a massive difference in getting the job you want and aspire to. Don't wait for recruiters and companies to come to you – go and find them. I'll show you how to do it.

Transforming Your LinkedIn Profile into a Career Magnet

Your LinkedIn profile needs to portray simply and clearly your true potential, make you stand out from the crowd and open the door to the job you want and deserve. The most important points to deal with and amend on your profile are the ones below.

LinkedIn Experience Sections: Complete a paragraph for each of your previous positions, and add the name and the logo of each company you have worked for. Adding the logo is possible only if the company has already set up a company page on LinkedIn and have uploaded the company logo to the page. It gives weight to your credibility to have the logo on display, especially if you have worked in the past for well-known companies.

Next, bring each experience section right up to date to make it easy for a prospective employer to see your employment journey and your previous roles and experience. If you don't display this information you could miss out job vacancy opportunities.

LinkedIn Headline and About Sections: Be clear on exactly what you are looking to do next. You can use the examples below as potential phrases to get a head start:

• I am looking for the next opportunity to (insert your relevant role description)

• I am seeking my next ideal job in (insert your relevant role description)

• I am available for (insert your relevant role description)

• I am searching for my next role as (insert your relevant role description)

Make sure to include easy searchable words in your LinkedIn headline and LinkedIn **About** sections relating to the position you are aiming for. In this way, when potential employers or recruiters search typing similar keywords they can find you.

Imagine no one knows you, what would your prospective employer want to see on your LinkedIn profile? Your information ought to be engaging in a way they will want to speak to you and find out more about you. Prospective employers would want to get to your CV – let's make it easy for them to see this.

How to Maximise Slideshare to Attract Employer Interest

You can upload your CV to Slideshare which at the click of a button can be positioned onto the summary section of your profile. By doing this, rather than uploading your CV from your desktop, you will be able to track how many people look at your CV using the Slideshare analytics. Here's how to do it.

Along the top black bar of your LinkedIn screen click the word **"Work"** and on the drop down menu click **"Slideshare"**. Slideshare will ask you to link your Slideshare and your LinkedIn accounts; have your LinkedIn password ready and Slideshare will be connected to your profile. Easy!

Save your CV as a pdf file or as a PowerPoint document on your desktop and upload it to Slideshare by clicking the orange **"Upload"** button on the top right hand side of your screen. Then click the orange **"Upload"** button in the middle of your Slideshare screen.

It is worth consulting an expert on getting your CV prepared in the best possible format because you may only get one chance to stand out from all the other candidates considered for the role.

Think of it in a similar way to your LinkedIn profile: what makes you different; what real expertise do you have; why should they employ you; what difference can you make if you get the job? Since you are not face to face with an employer to impress them in person, your personality and range of skills need to come across and shine through your CV.

Upload a file

Upload your CV file from your desktop and specify the category your information relates to. The category would be a word or word phrases relating to the area of expertise you are looking for a job in and which people can search through on Slideshare to find.

Next, title your document a CV and then add "Tags" – choose keywords relating to the job you are looking for – and don't forget to separate them by commas because they are searchable keywords. Have at least five tags, but you can add up to 20.

Last but not least, add a brief description of the document, explain that this is your CV and specify the persons you want to reach out to and the roles you are looking for. Have at least four sentences here for maximum visibility. Then click the orange **"Publish"** to upload your document onto the

Slideshare platform.

Once the document is uploaded, hover over your image on the top right hand corner of the screen, and on the drop down menu click **"My Uploads"**. Your uploaded CV will be visible; now hover over the document and you will be asked if you want to add the document directly to your LinkedIn profile. Click **"Yes"** and it will be added to the summary section. You can share your CV out across other social media platforms by clicking the buttons on the bottom of the document.

The more views you have on your CV the more opportunities will be coming your way as a result of generating more interest from within and out of LinkedIn. What's great about Slideshare is that you can track how often the document is viewed, where the viewer works, the country and the location it was viewed from, all of which is highly useful to know.

To track your statistics within Slideshare, hover over your image on the top right hand side of the screen and on the drop down menu click **"My Uploads"**. All your documents are shown in the most recent upload order. Click onto the document you want to view and at the bottom of the document, hover over the eye icon and then click the blue **"View Detailed Analytics"** wording.

You should check your stats regularly to see where the views are coming from and how well your CV is getting noticed. Best of all this service is for free!

View Detailed Analytics

The final part on your profile is to let know recruiters and companies looking for experts like you that you are open for job opportunities. Along the top black bar of your LinkedIn screen, click on the word **"Me"**. On the drop down menu click **"View profile"**, then scroll down to your private dashboard. Click on the **"Career interests"** wording and on the new screen click the button on the right hand side from **"Off"** to **"On"** position.

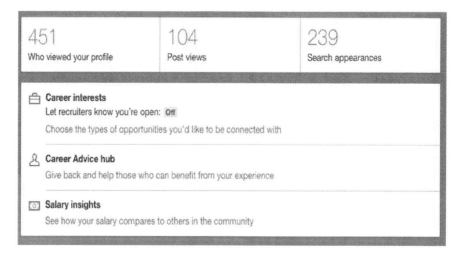

Fill in all the relevant information on job titles, geographical area, industries, size of company and you can hone in on roles that are being advertised on LinkedIn. Keep reading for more proactive ways to find that next new job.

Three Potent Tools to Help You Find the Work You Want

Now that you have made your LinkedIn profile as appealing as possible, it is time to think about putting together your strategy for finding a job. There are three ways to help you be successful in finding and securing your next role.

First, search for and connect to recruitment companies. Use LinkedIn's advanced search features to find local agencies and identify the type of recruitment they deal with. For example, if you are looking for an IT role you can search for local IT recruitment companies. Here's how.

Along the top black bar of your LinkedIn screen, click on the search box. A drop down menu will appear, click on the **"People"** button.

This will take you to a new screen where you can add all the relevant details for your search. You can start with the keyword; for example, I used Recruitment Solihull and this produced a list with 4,134 results. So a list of people will appear related to your particular research. Start sending requests to connect and then arrange to speak to the relevant people who, as recruiters, may have suitable positions on offer.

You can also repeat this exercise with the title of a person rather than a keyword. For example, you might want to connect to HR companies or recruitment specialists in a particular geographical area or field, for example, IT Recruitment. If you are searching for IT Recruitment, please make sure you type "IT Recruitment" in speech marks and then the geographical area you targeting otherwise LinkedIn will search both words as a phrase rather than individual words.

Second, identify particular companies you would like to work with. Search for their company page on LinkedIn and click the **"Follow"** button. You will see any job vacancies they post out from their LinkedIn company page and then apply accordingly.

You are also able to see the employees of that particular company on LinkedIn; find out if you are connected to any of them; or track down via one of your common connections the person you need to speak to. You then either connect to that person or ask one of your 1st line connections for an introduction and get the dialogue started. Here's how to find companies on LinkedIn.

Along the top black bar of your LinkedIn screen, click on the search box. On the drop down menu, click the **"Companies"** button.

Type in the name of the company you are looking for. If the company has set up a company page on LinkedIn its details will appear.

A company page is similar to having a website within LinkedIn. When viewing a company page, click the **"See all employees"** wording in blue and you can check out the list of employees and how you are connected to them. Click the blue **"Connect"** button to request them to join your network and once you acquire a new connection you should apply the same process; arrange a time to speak with them.

 2 connections work here. See all 3 employees →

Third, look through your connections' connections and ask for introductions to people they know. This is where it is very useful to have built up a good set of connections you know well enough to ask for introductions. Some of my best clients have come from me asking my 1st line connections for introductions to people they know. Here's how this works.

Search for one of your 1st line LinkedIn connections by typing their name in the search box on the top black bar of your LinkedIn screen, and then scroll down their LinkedIn profile. Positioned on the left hand side of their LinkedIn profile, under their headline, you will find "**Highlights**".

Highlights

1,299 mutual connections
You and Peter both know Dan Mogg, Andy Bull, and 1,297 others

Click on the words **"mutual connections"** and a list of their 1st line connections will appear. I have found that if you know your 1st line connection person well, he or she would be happy to help you with connecting to you people they know. When you have identified such a person, go to the Messaging section within LinkedIn (located on the top black bar of your screen next to the Notifications flag icon).

Click the email button (the blue square with the pencil icon), type the name of your 1st line connection and send an email asking kindly to connect you together. Your 1st line connection can reply to your email and by copying in the person you want to connect to, it will get the introduction started. Very easy and very effective!

Messaging	🖉	New message
🔍 Search messages ☰		Pardip Singhota ✕ Matt Wallis ✕

These three ways are part of your proactive approach to finding prospective employers and landing your dream job on LinkedIn. Next, you will learn how to hone your job hunting skills to find and apply for jobs directly.

The final part of this chapter is about helping you hone your job search within LinkedIn in much more detail to get even more precise and targeted job locating results.

Utilising LinkedIn to Find a Job Ahead of Your Competitors

Jobs search feature is one of the most useful parts of using LinkedIn to search for a particular type of job and apply for it directly through LinkedIn. Most people have never heard of, let alone used this search button, and it is another hidden gem you can use to great advantage.

The **"Jobs"** button is found along the top black bar of your LinkedIn screen on the left hand side of the word Messaging.

Click on it and you will be taken to a new screen. You can now search by job title, keywords or company name.

If you know exactly the type of role you are looking for then search for a job title and, similarly, search for a particular company by name. A wider but less focussed search would be to search using keywords. A list of jobs will appear on the new screen; however you need to hone the search in order to find your ideal role.

On the top of your screen you can start filtering the information including geographical area, selecting a certain company; the date the job was posted, from anytime through to the past 24 hours; the experience level, from entry level through to director level. You can also select a type of industry or choose a job function.

From this search screen you can create a job alert based on your set criteria, LinkedIn will alert you to any new job opportunities that become available. Click the **"Job Alert"** button to activate this.

Choose a daily or weekly alert and how you want to be notified – be it via email or mobile and desktop. Click the blue **"Save"** button to save the alert. It's how you can keep a regular eye on any new positions being posted which would match your chosen criteria and location.

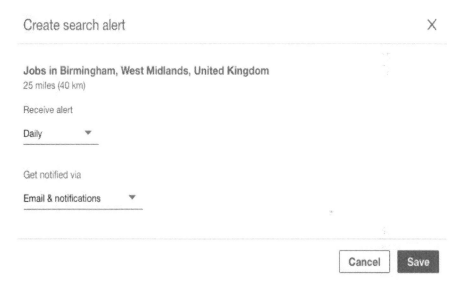

For more detailed results, you can take your job search to the next level with Premium Career, which is a paid premium service. There are six additional benefits.

One: Direct messaging to recruiters. Reach out to any recruiter or job advertisers using three InMail credits feature. You can send three messages directly to someone on LinkedIn without being a connection.

Two: Featured Applicant. You will appear at the top of the list which will increase your visibility and help you stand out.

Three: Online video courses. Improve your technical and creative skills taught by industry leaders available on LinkedIn Learning.

Four: Who's Viewed Your Profile. Discover who has viewed your LinkedIn profile within the last three months and how they found you.

Five: Applicant Insights. See how you compare to other candidates. You can compare by top skills, seniority level, education and other features so you can apply with confidence.

Six: Instant access to salary insights. See salary details when hunting for jobs without sharing your personal data..

To try the Premium Careers version you need to add your credit card details, but you can cancel before the end of the one month free trial. It is worth going for the free trial before you make any commitments – you may have found your ideal job before a month is out!

To set up the Premium version, click on your photograph along the top black bar of LinkedIn. On the drop down menu click **"Try Premium Free for 1 month"**. Click the **"Explore all plans"** button and on the new screen click **"Select plan"** in the Career box. At the bottom of the screen click the blue **"Start my free month"** button.

Start my free month

Or go along the black bar of your LinkedIn screen and on the top right hand side of your screen click **"Try Upgrade to Premium"**.

On the new screen you will see the options available. Click **"Explore all plans"** to set up and you are good to go.

Booster Tip: You can save the jobs you are interested in to consider them later on. You can also save your searches, thus LinkedIn will speed up the process and let you know of any new results that match your criteria. You can also review your past job applications to keep track of how they are progressing.

It is really easy to apply online for advertised jobs through LinkedIn. When you see your ideal position from your list, click the blue **"Apply"** button located in the Job description section. You can also click the **"Save"** button to save the job to look at later.

Save   Apply

You can upload your CV by clicking the blue **"Browse files"** wording and once the files are uploaded, click the blue **"Submit application"** button to apply. For your peace of mind, your job searching activity on LinkedIn is private; no one else on LinkedIn can see what jobs and positions you have applied for.

Apply to CV-Library Ltd

Dawn Adlam

LinkedIn Training ▶ Helping Sales Teams connect to their next biggest client & generate profits ▶ Workshops ▶ Coaching

Birmingham, United Kingdom

Review profile

Email

dawn@thebizlinks.com ▼

Phone

+44 7880 725564

Resume (optional)

Upload

Microsoft Word or PDF only (5MB)

We include a copy of your full profile with your application

Learn what we do with your resume

☑ **Follow CV-Library Ltd**

Cancel   **Submit application**

Having success with the job hunting is not just about having an appealing LinkedIn profile and uploading your CV. It's about using LinkedIn as an online directory to be proactive in searching and applying for jobs you want and that are right for you. Use this alongside following the companies you want to work for and also connect to relevant recruitment and or HR people.

Keep positive and good things will happen, my motto is don't give up because there is always a way. You are already putting in some great effort on LinkedIn if you have come this far. Your ideal job is out there waiting for you – go and find it, and find it you will!

In the next part I will be sharing more tips on improving your LinkedIn profile to get noticed. With access to tens of millions of LinkedIn users you need to look as strong and professional as possible to get a massive head start in getting that visibility.

Part V
Stronger And Healthier LinkedIn Profile And Presence

12

How to Clean Up Your LinkedIn Profile for Maximum Results

A crucial part of being successful on LinkedIn is maintaining your LinkedIn profile to a healthy state. As your LinkedIn network grows, there are always issues that come with it and which, if unchecked, do affect your LinkedIn performance and can lead to a huge waste of time and effort. That's why it is important to make sure you regularly check you are free from connections you do not want in your network or that are not active. Furthermore, by keeping a tab on the groups you are in makes it easy for you to leave the groups that are not a good fit for you or they are dormant.

There are many issues about managing one's profile LinkedIn users need to tackle on a daily basis, but the most commonly asked questions, which I'll cover in this section, are:

• How to remove connections you don't want anymore

• What to do if you have set up two different personal LinkedIn profiles

• What happens if you have joined the wrong or an inactive LinkedIn group

• How to leave LinkedIn completely

How to Remove a LinkedIn Connection

There are many reasons why you would want to remove some of your connections: they might be a direct competitor; they might bombard you with sales messages (you can report this to LinkedIn if it gets too much); you might have connected to them by mistake and so on. Whatever the reason, you should remove such connections because what you don't want is to clog up your database with connections you are not benefitting or getting value from in terms of your business or your personal growth.

There are two ways to remove a LinkedIn connection: from your own connections hub; or from their profile.

To remove a connection from your own LinkedIn connections hub, go to the top black bar of your LinkedIn screen and click **"My Network"**. Once inside the hub, click **"Connections"** which is under the the Manage my network section.

Manage my network

  Connections   6,739

A list of your connections will appear with your most recent connections first. Search for the person you want to remove by clicking on the search button on the right hand side of your screen, then type in his or her name. When you find the connection, click on the three dots you will find on the right hand side of the **"Message"** box. On the dropdown list that appears, click **"Remove connection"** and that LinkedIn connection will disappear from your network.

To remove a connection from their LinkedIn profile, first you go along the top black bar of your LinkedIn screen and type in the white search box the name of the connection you want to remove.

Once you are on their profile, click on the **"More..."** box which is next to the Message box, and on the drop down menu that appears, click on the wording **"Remove Connection"**.

And don't worry, because in either case the connections you are removing will not know they have been removed and neither will your wider network. They will no longer be a 1st connection or appear in your contacts section. But, remember, once you have removed a connection their endorsements and recommendation will be removed from your profile and won't be reinstated even if you re-establish the connection. Only the member who breaks the connection can re-establish it.

Avoiding LinkedIn Duplicate Accounts

I come across this often: people have set up two LinkedIn profiles often by mistake (and occasionally deliberately!). Having two profiles can confuse people and makes it difficult for them to contact you especially if one profile has an out of date email; you will never get their messages and opportunities could easily be missed. What's more, LinkedIn only allow one profile per person so it is crucial to remove the duplicate account.

You can do a search for your name in the white search box along the top black bar and see if more than one profile shows up. If you are not aware of having another LinkedIn account you may get a message that says the email address you're attempting to use to login is associated with another account, and this can happen if you use a number of different email addresses. At this point you need to take action to merge both the accounts.

It is easy to identify your actual account; the profile with the **YOU** icon is the account where you're currently signed in. A profile containing your information that doesn't have a **YOU** icon is a duplicate account. Here's how to merge duplicate LinkedIn accounts.

Along the top black bar of your LinkedIn screen, click the word **"Me"**. On the drop down menu that appears click on the **"Open Quick Help"** wording underneath the NEED HELP? section.

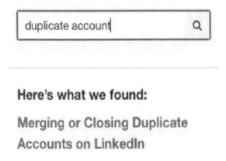

Type in the search box "duplicate accounts" and click the search button. Click on the relevant answer and follow the instructions to merge the connections from one account to the other and close the duplicate one down.

Don't delay doing this. Once you find you have a duplicate account get this sorted as soon as possible, it really keeps things simple for everyone in your network.

How to Leave a LinkedIn Group

Being part of the LinkedIn community via groups should be a major part of your LinkedIn activity to get noticed and show your expertise. But along the way you might find a number of reasons to leave a LinkedIn group you are part of. It could be the group hasn't grown in members, it is inactive, it may have nothing to do with your business, you may have joined it as part of your strategy to message someone you are not connected to or you joined by mistake.

What's more, there's no point gathering groups for the sake of it, you will get deluged with useless emails or, even worse, waste your time in discussions that have no value; believe me, there are far too many going around.

Here's how to leave a group.

Along the top black bar of your LinkedIn screen, click the word **"Work"** and on the drop down menu click **"Groups"**.

A list of the groups you manage and those you are in will appear. Click on the group you want to leave and once inside the group click on the three grey dots and on the drop down menu click **"Leave this group"**.

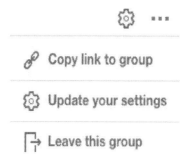

How to Close a LinkedIn Account

This is different to having a duplicate LinkedIn profile, this is an option to close your account completely and delete your profile. By doing so, you remove access to all your LinkedIn information from the LinkedIn site. Before closing your account, please check the following:

• You won't have access to your connections or any information you've added to your account

• Your profile will no longer be visible on LinkedIn

• Search engines such as Yahoo!, Bing, and Google may still display your information temporarily due to the way they collect and update their search data

• You will lose all recommendations and endorsements you've collected on your LinkedIn profile

• If you have a premium membership, own a LinkedIn group, or have a premium account license, you will have to resolve those accounts before being able to close your basic account

To close your account, go along the top black bar of your LinkedIn screen and click the word **"Me"**. On the drop down menu click "**Settings & Privacy"**, then click on the **"Account"** button on the left hand side. Click on **"Account management"**.

Scroll down the page and choose **"Closing your LinkedIn account"**. Give the reason you want to close your account and then click **"Next"**. Enter your password and click **"Close account"**.

Closing your LinkedIn account

Learn about your options, and close your account if you wish

If you have a premium membership, set up your own a LinkedIn group or have a premium account license you will have to resolve those accounts before being able to close your basic account. At this point, you have reached the end of your LinkedIn journey so, please make sure you want to go ahead with this.

If you want answers for other enquiries you can use LinkedIn's Help Center. On the top black bar of LinkedIn screen, click **"Me"**. On the drop down menu that appears, click on **"Open Quick Help"** wording underneath NEED HELP? section.

NEED HELP?

Open Quick Help

Enter your own questions in the white question box and click the looking glass icon on the right hand side of the box. It's as simple as that.

If you cannot find the answer to a particular question, you can email LinkedIn which will open up a ticket to track your query. To do this you need to go to the Help Center page again and, as above, click **"Go to Help Homepage"**. Click next on the **"Visit Help Forum"**; it has many questions and answers from users you might be interested in reading.

 Popular actions

Visit our Help Forum
View, ask, or answer questions about using LinkedIn. Our moderators and community can help!

Visit Help Forum

Right at the bottom of this page (in very small writing!) you will see the **"Contact us"** wording. Click it.

Linked**in**   Contact us

Click the **"Get help from us"** box. You will need to complete the relevant sections about your query and, once completed, click the blue **"Submit"** button. It is usually dealt with within 24 hours.

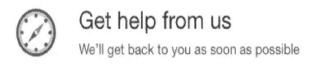

Get help from us
We'll get back to you as soon as possible

So there you have it, the most frequently asked questions about polishing one's LinkedIn profile. I hope these have been useful so you can be aware of and avoid the potential pitfalls alongside building and maintaining your LinkedIn profile and keeping your connections in good shape.

13

The Real Truth about LinkedIn Changes and How to Keep Up with Them

LinkedIn is a powerful social networking platform both as a tool for serious professionals and as an online B2B directory; in fact, it is the largest business orientated directory in the world. Though LinkedIn's functionality and features are being updated and improved all the time, your professional LinkedIn profile has not been affected – all the basic elements to it are still the same.

What's more, in December 2016, Microsoft bought LinkedIn for more than $26 billion! This means that Microsoft will make more changes now by integrating LinkedIn into every platform and piece of software they own from Word, Excel, SharePoint to Outlook and Notepad and even PowerPoint. Such powerful integration provides the ultimate storehouse – the master personnel file room in the house – and how cool is that? A truly global giant linking together professional online business communities and changing the way businesses and professionals like you come together and interact.

So relax and don't worry; whatever changes there have been or may be in the future, your personal LinkedIn profile and your LinkedIn strategy will not go out of fashion. Instead, they will only evolve and get better as additional technology and benefits are applied to LinkedIn. Here are some of the key changes.

LinkedIn's most recent changes relate to the look and layout of the Home page and the Advanced search facility – the "activity" part of using LinkedIn. Other already existing benefits have been Slideshare and the cool option of adding a background photograph, for example. LinkedIn's main Home page, the place where LinkedIn users hang out on a daily basis, is regularly updated from a cosmetic perspective to keep it fresh. Some of the buttons may move around and extra benefits may be introduced. For example, when one of your 1st line connections makes a new LinkedIn connection you now have the opportunity to connect to that particular new connection directly should you wish to do so.

Another recent change is that you cannot see any longer on the Home page when your connections recommend each other, but you can still see this information in situ on their profile. If you spend time regularly on LinkedIn's Home page, it is easy to see the slight modifications along the way.

The Advanced search facility has recently changed for the users who don't pay the Premium version of LinkedIn; there is now a percentage limit on how many people you can search for each month. Don't worry though; this limit reverts back on the first day of each month so you can start searching again. Take a look at the super booster tips in Chapter 16 to see how to work within this limitation if you run out searches. You can still search to find people or businesses and just about anything LinkedIn related by using names, keywords and locations, but not by postcode anymore.

LinkedIn will alert you with any major changes along the way – you will see text boxes asking you to take a look around the new layouts. I keep an eye regularly for any changes that happen. I email my connections and followers who are subscribed to Popcorn, I publish LinkedIn posts advising of those changes and also share regular updates on the LinkedIn Home page.

What's more, more than 80% of the sections in this book will not be affected by LinkedIn's updates and changes. Of the less than 20% part of the book, the section that is likely to change would be the functionality of the marketing side of LinkedIn. I will keep you abreast of any new system changes that may affect the rest of the book; so you don't need to worry about being left behind!

14

Facts You Should Know about LinkedIn Premium to Help You Decide on Upgrading for Top Results from Your LinkedIn Activity

Upgrading or not to a LinkedIn Premium account is one of the most frequently asked questions by those who attend my LinkedIn workshops and seminars. I say it is best you use the basic version until you know it inside out and then consider one of the LinkedIn Premium version options. Even in my case, being a LinkedIn coach, I only use the basic version of LinkedIn because it does do everything I need to get done.

I have found that most of the users of the LinkedIn Premium versions are recruiters and sales directors and managers. These are people who want access to more metrics and reach more people quicker, but this is not the case for most LinkedIn users.

Booster Tip: You can try the Premium version of LinkedIn for a month for free, but to do so you will need to add your credit card details. You can however cancel before the end of the month and no payment will be taken from your account.

Let's look at the options available to help you make an informed decision as to the best version for you and if it is worth going for. Along the top black bar of your LinkedIn screen, on the far right hand side, click the wording **"Try Premium Free for 1 month"** . You will be taken to a new screen which will show the paid premium versions that are available.

Each LinkedIn premium plan is priced out differently to suit the features and benefits it offers, with a free trial for each. First, get a better idea as to what you want to achieve with each upgraded package plan by analysing the information below. Click **"Explore all plans"** and you get four options.

Dawn, how would you like Premium to help?
We'll recommend the right plan for you.

◯ To job search with confidence and get hired

◯ To grow my network or manage my reputation

◯ To find leads more effectively

◯ To find and hire talent faster

Explore all plans

Land Your Dream Job

This will help if you want to job search with confidence and get hired, to grow your network or manage your reputation.

Career: This package is ideal if you are looking for a job and there are three benefits for choosing this plan:

- Stand out from your competition and get in front of hiring managers

- See how you compare to other candidates

- Learn new skills to advance your career

It gives six main benefits:

- Direct messaging to any recruiter or job poster with three inMail credits.

- Featured applicant, stand out more when you apply as a featured applicant.

- Online video courses for the most in-demand business, tech and creative skills taught by top experts.

- Who's viewed your profile in the last 90 days and how they found you.

- Applicant insights – see how you fare to other candidates.

- Instant access to salary insights when browsing jobs.

Expanding Your Network

Business: This package is useful if you are looking to grow your network quickly and it offers three main benefits:

- Find and contact the right people

• Promote and grow your business

• Learn new skills to kick-start your professional brand

It gives six main benefits:

• 15 InMail messages to contact anyone LinkedIn.

• Business insights into a company's growth and trends.

• Online video courses for the most in-demand business, tech and creative skills taught by LinkedIn learning.

• Who's viewed your profile in the last 90 days.

• Unlimited profile browsing up to 3rd line connections.

• Career insights – see how you compare to other job applicants and get instant access to salary details.

Open Up Sales Opportunities

This will help you find leads more effectively.

Sales: This package is suitable if you want to or are responsible for generating new leads and sales.

Sales Navigator Professional features

20 InMail™ messages
Start meaningful conversations with prospects, even if you're not connected

Sales Insights
Get insights on your accounts and leads, like job changes, company growth, and more

Advanced Search with Lead Builder
Zero in on decision makers and create custom lead lists with advanced search filters

Who's Viewed Your Profile
See what prospects have been interested in you over the last 90 days

Unlimited people browsing
View unlimited profiles from search results and suggested profiles – up to 3rd degree

Lead recommendations and saved leads
Quickly discover the right people and save them to stay up to date

It gives six main benefits:

• 20 InMail Messages. Start conversations with prospects even if you are not connected.

• Sales Insights. Get real time insights on your accounts and leads on job changes, company growth and more.

• Advanced Search with Lead Builder. Zero in on decision makers and create custom lead lists with advanced search features.

• Who's Viewed Your Profile. See what prospects have been interested in you over the last 90 days.

• Unlimited people browsing. View unlimited profiles from search results and suggested profiles up to 3rd degree connections.

• Lead recommendations and saved leads. Discover the right people in key positions and save them.

With the sales navigator plan you have 20 InMail available to send out each month which means you can contact and message 20 people on LinkedIn directly. You can use this as a tool to start prospecting with people you don't know. You can see who has viewed your profile in the last 90 days; see also the number of potential prospects who have been interested in you. The free version of LinkedIn only allows you to see the last five people.

Using the advanced search in conjunction with Lead Builder helps you hone in on decision makers and create custom lead lists with certain search filters. You can view an unlimited list of LinkedIn profiles from the search results – up to 3rd degree connections. You can get relevant sales insights on your accounts and leads to help you build relationships. Account pages help you focus on your target accounts with company updates and information tailored to you. Also, you can use TeamLink to find colleagues who can introduce you to people at the targeted account.

Spotting and Hiring Bright Talent

This will help a great deal to find and hire top talent faster.

Hiring: This package is crucial if you are a recruiter.

There are eight main benefits:

• 30 InMail Messages. Contact anyone and save time with templates.

• Advanced Search. Zero in on top talent with advanced search filters designed for recruiting.

• Smart Suggestions. Use dynamic suggestions as you search to uncover additional talent.

• Integrated hiring. Manage your whole candidate pool in one place.

• Who's Viewed Your Profile. See potential candidates who viewed your profile in the last 90 days.

• Unlimited people browsing. View unlimited profiles from search results and suggested profiles up to 3rd degree connections.

• Automatic candidate tracking. Track candidates and open roles with projects.

• Recruiting – specific design. The LinkedIn experience, enhanced for recruiting.

With the Integrated hiring you can manage your whole candidate pool in one place and organize them in folders and set reminders to follow up. You have an open profile so anyone on LinkedIn can see your full profile, in that way candidates can find and reach out to you. There is also a Recruiter Mobile option which helps you find top talent anywhere and anytime whilst out and about.

To purchase any of these four premium packages click the **"Start my free month"** button at the bottom of each screen.

Start my free month

You can downgrade or cancel any of the premium versions at any time at www.linkedin.com/settings. Also, you can pay monthly or annually and there's 20% off if you pay upfront for annual subscriptions.

So there you have it, all the information about upgrading or not to a LinkedIn Premium account at your fingertips. Try out the free trial and then weigh the cost against other marketing expenses and the time you need to put in. Is it worth paying the monthly fee or you can achieve the same or similar outcome using the basic version? Decide and off you go!

It's time to learn tips and hints to help you make the most of face to face networking. Because you are now ready take what you have learnt from the online world experience and put it into practice when engaging with people out there, in person, in the real world.

15

Taking Your LinkedIn Network Offline to Promote Your Brand and Build Solid and Durable Business Relationships

---

Face to face networking can be a really daunting task for most people. When I started attending business networking events I was nervous and had no confidence approaching and talking to people. I didn't want to catch anyone's eye and was lost for words because this was different to socialising with friends. What do you say to a room full of people whom you have never met before?

To say I looked like a wallflower it is an understatement. If you told me back then I would end up on stage presenting to hundreds of people, I would say you were dreaming! But it is true; now I love meeting, networking and helping as many people as I can.

The main misconception about networking is that you turn up to a room full of people eager to give you business, or you go to networking events to sell to people. It is not true. The reality is that people attending are as nervous as you and a way to tackle nervousness is talk about themselves. This may look as they are trying to convince you to buy from them which can come across as selling.

Having been an active networker for over ten years I have learnt one valuable lesson: engaging with others is good and asking questions is even better; but trying to sell isn't. If you have ever had a business card thrust into your hand before any conversation has taken place, you know what I mean. As you know, the majority of people don't bite.

I have met many friendly people I could relate to, I shared interests with and who were good listeners and genuinely interested in me and my services. The foundation of my networking has always been to look for, find and engage with such people.

Your approach to networking both in person and via LinkedIn should be the same. The best networkers don't do the talking; instead they ask questions, listen and find out how they can help. The first questions you should ask when introduced to a new person should be, *"Tell me about your business"* and *"How can I help you?"*

By letting other people do the talking it helps you find out more about them and their business so you can respond by either filling their business needs or introducing them to other people in your network who can help.

Here are my top eight tips for getting the most out of any networking event and finding new people you can help and build long term strategic alliances with.

One: Discover the event that suits you

There are many types of networking events: weekly, fortnightly, monthly, lunchtime, early morning, early evening, formal, informal and relaxed, ladies only, industry specific, LinkedIn face to face meetings and so on. Most will have a structure. Try different types of networking events and find the ones that suit you from the point of view of time, location, format and the people attending each event.

Two: Plan ahead

Being late rarely makes a good impression so make sure you know where the venue and plan your journey well ahead. Check out the local car parking areas if parking isn't available at the venue. If it is a paid networking event, bring cash with you. Ask for the attendee list ahead of the event so you can select who you want to speak with.

Three: Set goals

Your goals maybe different to mine, and unless you set yourself a reason to attend you may well be wasting time and money turning up. Decide beforehand what you want to achieve from attending a networking event.

Turning up only once is unlikely to generate a new client unless someone has an urgent need for your services. Do you want to make five new contacts you can add to your network on LinkedIn or arrange a meeting with someone new who would make a good strategic alliance partner? Be specific as to what you want to walk away with.

Four: First impression matters

What you wear depends on the type of networking event and the attendees. A more formal event usually dictates suit and tie, a more relaxed event is likely to need a more casual style. Remember, you will be meeting new people and the first impression you want to make is crucial. Personal hygiene is important, too. Clean hair and clothes along with breath fresheners and a not too overpowering scent will give you extra confidence and leave a lasting impression.

Five: Networking tools

Bring along business cards. Approaching someone and saying, "Hello, here's my card!" is not the right thing to do. But if you want to follow up with someone, make it easy for him or her to contact you afterwards by offering your business card .

Always keep a pen handy to make notes on the back of business cards you receive during the event whist the conversation is fresh in your mind. With large numbers at a networking event you might not remember all the people you need to follow up with, so making notes along the way will help jog your memory afterwards. Always take a smile with you – no one wants to speak to miserable people!

Six: How to start a conversation

This can be a sticking point if you are not confident in a room full of strangers. People love talking about themselves (some in great detail!), so go armed with a handful of questions you can ask to keep the conversation going. Here are some proven and tested questions:

What do you do? Where do you work? Who would make a good connection for you? What type of clients are you looking for? What do you most enjoy about your job? Tell me about your Business. How can I help you?

Booster Tip: If you get stuck in a corner with one person, remove yourself from conversations politely (say you need to replenish your drink; it always works) and mingle with other people.

Seven: Follow up

Following up after the event is the most important part of networking. Always do what you promise you will do. It could be calling someone, sending over a proposal, emailing across information and so on. To get a good working relationship off to the best possible start always, always follow up on the actions you promised – it is the fastest and surest way to build trust and lead to new business opportunities.

Eight: Arrange face to face meetings

Once you have followed up with and identified the people who would make good strategic partnerships (by this I mean people you have a similar client base and could work together) you arrange a meeting so you can get to know them better. Surrounding yourself with people you know, like and trust is a powerful way to generate new business for each other.

The easiest way to get started is to look for networking events around your area. Do your research on what type of events there are, select one, book a place and turn up. What's the worst that can happen? Being a part of BNI, for example, catapulted my business and has generated me tens of thousands of pounds and I still have those relationships active ten years on and the people I meet regularly become part of my extended "sales team".

Someone once told me to feel the fear and do it anyway! It can be difficult if networking doesn't come naturally to you or you haven't tried it before. But until you take that step through the door you will never know. Be brave and try it. In your first meeting, as you walk into the room you may be thinking what the heck you are doing there. You'll be amazed at how genuine and welcoming people are. Find the right group of people and you and your business will be unstoppable, and you'll never look back.

16

Bonus Booster Tips

I have brought together 22 of the best golden nuggets I myself use to get the most out of LinkedIn. By dipping in and out when as you need to will save you time and help you achieve more with your LinkedIn activity. I have grouped them in four parts and ordered them starting with your LinkedIn profile and then moving onto your LinkedIn marketing and strategy. No cheating though – don't forget to read the rest of the book first!

Keeping Your LinkedIn Profile Simple

Booster Tip 1: Create your About section in a Word document first, so you can make sure you correct spelling mistakes and grammar; they make your profile look very unprofessional.

Booster Tip 2: By connecting your Twitter account to your LinkedIn profile you can save yourself lots of time by sending tweets out with a click of the button from LinkedIn.

Booster Tip 3: This will save you time when asking for recommendations. Write out your personal message in a Word document or Evernote first. But make sure to leave enough space in the middle of the request for three value questions to guide the person write a recommendation based on your professional values.

Booster Tip 4: By alerting your network to your profile changes you will appear in their notifications hub increasing your visibility and helps you get noticed more on LinkedIn.

Booster Tip 5: If you add an icon to your headline (I use an arrow) please make sure there is a space before and after the icon otherwise the word will not be recognised in LinkedIn searches.

LinkedIn Marketing Cues to Help Clients Buy from You

Booster Tip 1: Always have a call to action at the bottom of your document to help direct the reader take the action you want them to, once they have read it. For example, *"Take action now for a free website overview"* or *"Special offer this month: half price printing of 500 business cards"* and so on.

Booster Tip 2: For further outreach you can add a company button, which is a hyperlink directly linked to your LinkedIn company page. Think about adding this to your email footer or blog or website with a message such as , *"Click here to follow our Company Page on LinkedIn for regular Industry updates."*

Booster Tip 3: Showcase company pages are useful if you offer multiple services. For example, if you are a web design company you might offer website design, SEO and so on. Create a series of Showcase pages where you can share further content, start building relationships and separate out your services so you can cross sell from the company page.

Booster Tip 4: Your company domain (email address) can only be used once to set up a LinkedIn company page, and you can only have on page relating to your business. An alternative to this is setting up a new LinkedIn group relating to your company services. This means you can communicate with a targeted group of people in your LinkedIn group rather than with the followers on a LinkedIn company page. Your LinkedIn group will be on view to LinkedIn members at the bottom of your profile.

Booster Tip 5: If you mention a 1st line connection on an update on the Home page, as you start typing their name use the @ symbol and the name will be highlighted in blue so anyone viewing the Home page can click on their name and be directed to their profile.

Booster Tip 6: When you create and publish your own LinkedIn articles, LinkedIn displays them in chronological order at the top of your LinkedIn profile, just underneath your About section. This brings your profile to life and helps position you as the expert in your field. By creating a series of LinkedIn posts you'll be recognised as an expert in your field.

Booster Tip 7: At the push of a button you can quickly share your article out to LinkedIn and Twitter for a wider outreach. You are thus on your way to creating a bank of material you can go back to any time to edit, update and post out regularly to keep in touch with your followers.

Booster Tip 8: The final part of creating an article is to add three #Hashtags, which should be relevant searchable words and have replaced the previous Tags. #Hashtags can be searched on mobile devices for additional visibility and Chrome seems to be the most compatible browser to create your LinkedIn articles in for extra searchability.

Booster Tip 9: The same as in your LinkedIn profile headline, your key searchable words need to be used in the headline of your LinkedIn article. By using keywords you increase your visibility for people searching for your services.

Booster Tip 10: Hashtags can help your content reach a wider audience on LinkedIn similar to Twitter and Instagram. Always add three to five hashtags to your Posts to categorise the content and create niche hashtags suitable for your brand.

LinkedIn Strategy Nuggets

Booster Tip 1: Located underneath your headline (and everyone else's headline) there is the Connections section. Here you can search through your 1st line connections to find out who they know who would be good introductions for you.

Booster Tip 2: If you want to search a keyword phrase you should link the words together using speech marks, otherwise LinkedIn will search both words independently and this will make the search far too wide.

Booster Tip 3: It is worth noting you only have a percentage of searches each month on the basic version of LinkedIn so always type a location to keep the search to a minimum. Your search volume is reset on the first of every month.

Booster Tip 4: You can save the jobs you are interested in to look at later, you can also save job searches. LinkedIn will speed up the search process and will let you know of any new results that match your criteria. You can also review your past job applications to keep track of how they are progressing.

Booster Tip 5: When looking a LinkedIn member's profile, take a look on the right hand side of your screen – the People Also Viewed list. LinkedIn algorithms would suggest other people you can connect to and it is based on the type of profiles you are looking at, and this is a great way to prospect for similar new connections.

Booster Tip 6: You can try the Premium version of LinkedIn for a month for free, but to do so you will need to add your credit card details. You can however cancel before the end of the month and no payment will be taken from your account.

Face to Face Networking Rescue Hints

Booster Tip: If you get stuck in a corner with one person, remove yourself from conversations politely (say you need to replenish your drink; it always works) and mingle with other people. Also, always follow up after the networking event with people you met up because following up is the key to generating new clients.

Printed in Great Britain
by Amazon

64746714R00106